Grinnell Clark
Dublin
N.H.
'44
July
from H.A.
Yeomans

FACTS AND VISIONS

LONDON : HUMPHREY MILFORD
OXFORD UNIVERSITY PRESS

A. Lawrence Lowell.

FACTS AND VISIONS
TWENTY-FOUR BACCALAUREATE SERMONS

By ABBOTT LAWRENCE LOWELL

EDITED BY HENRY AARON YEOMANS

1944
HARVARD UNIVERSITY PRESS
Cambridge, Massachusetts

COPYRIGHT, 1944
BY THE PRESIDENT AND FELLOWS OF HARVARD COLLEGE

THIS BOOK IS PRODUCED IN FULL COMPLIANCE WITH
THE GOVERNMENT'S REGULATIONS FOR CONSERVING
PAPER AND OTHER ESSENTIAL MATERIALS.

PRINTED AT THE HARVARD UNIVERSITY PRINTING OFFICE
CAMBRIDGE, MASSACHUSETTS, U.S.A.

PREFACE

FOR TWENTY-FOUR successive years the graduating class in Harvard College asked President Lowell to address them at their Baccalaureate Sunday service, that is, to preach their Baccalaureate sermon. He never thought of himself as a preacher and seldom talked or wrote of religious values, but he never refused. Underneath his genial austerity he was the ardent friend of all college men everywhere, a friend who was betting his life's work on their value to the community. He was, too, a devoutly religious man. If the Seniors wanted him to preach he would preach; and, if he preached, he must preach of the heart kept with diligence, for out of it are the issues of life.

As his religion was universal, there is in his sermons nothing denominational or sectarian. He thought the most devout worshipper he had ever seen was a lone Mahometan prone on the floor of Santa Sophia. As his religion was above all else practical, although ritual and dogma did not disturb him they mattered little except as aids to conduct. In the best and the one essential meaning of the word he was a Puritan; for him every act had a moral significance which alone gave it lasting importance. He was always looking for the vision, but the vision he sought was a vision of right conduct. Moreover, it was a vision which he could see only by looking at and through the facts. He thought the visionary did more harm than the rascal.

These sermons are the unpretentious words of a man of action with a strong religious conscience, saying farewell to a group who had enjoyed extraordinary privileges and owed a corresponding debt to the public. He was talking to them as Gonsalvo de Cordova spoke to his knights who had prided themselves on holding their own against the French. "I sent you out," said the Great Captain, "for better men."

Lowell, of course, did not mean to limit the application of what he said to the privileged group whom his hearers represented. The principles he drove home year after year he thought should be the commonplaces of every man's life. In theory, he almost assumed them; in applying them to conduct he gave his best in these sermons. The language is so simple as to be almost deceptive; but any reader who thinks there is anything trivial in the substance had better read again.

H. A. Y.

CAMBRIDGE
FEBRUARY, 1944

CONTENTS

			PAGE
I	*June 19, 1910*	GEN. 32:24, 26	3
II	*June 18, 1911*	EZEK. 33:6	12
III	*June 16, 1912*	LUKE 16:11, 12	20
IV	*June 15, 1913*	I SAM. 17:55	29
V	*June 14, 1914*	II KINGS 13:14–19	34
VI	*June 20, 1915*	MATT. 6:22	42
VII	*June 18, 1916*	I COR. 3:13–15	48
VIII	*June 17, 1917*	II SAM. 5:24	55
IX	*June 16, 1918*	HEB. 11:1–12:1	61
X	*June 15, 1919*	I COR. 15:29	68
XI	*June 20, 1920*	JONAH 1:1, 2	75
XII	*June 19, 1921*	ISAIAH 5:20, 21; WISDOM 6:24	83
XIII	*June 18, 1922*	II COR. 10:12	90
XIV	*June 17, 1923*	I COR. 3:11–15	99
XV	*June 15, 1924*	LUKE 22:35, 36	106
XVI	*June 14, 1925*	PSALM 121:6	113
XVII	*June 20, 1926*	PSALM 24:1, 2	120
XVIII	*June 19, 1927*	ECCL. 1:3	126
XIX	*June 17, 1928*	MATT. 6:22, 23	135
XX	*June 16, 1929*	DEUT. 6:10–12	138
XXI	*June 15, 1930*	WISDOM 9:1–4	145
XXII	*June 14, 1931*	ECCL. 9:16, 18	153
XXIII	*June 19, 1932*	II KINGS 7:1–2, 6–7, 16–17	161
XXIV	*June 18, 1933*	LUKE 21:9–11, 19	168

FACTS AND VISIONS

Facts and Visions

June 19, 1910

And Jacob was left alone; and there wrestled a man with him until the breaking of the day.

And he said, Let me go, for the day breaketh. And he said, I will not let thee go, except thou bless me.

GENESIS 32:24, 26.

IN THE graphic chapters in which the Jewish writers sketched the life of the founder of their race we are told of two dreams or visions that left deep traces on his mind. One of them came to him when he first left his father's home, and went forth into the world to seek his fortune. As he slept upon the ground he dreamt that God appeared to him, assured him of his protection, and promised him prosperity. There is a note of youthful buoyancy about him, a tone of confidence as he seeks to make a compact with the Almighty about the future. The second vision came when he journeyed back years later, bringing with him the flocks and herds he had acquired, but uncertain whether he would not after all be ruined by the vengeance of Esau, his brother, whom he had supplanted in their father's blessing. It came to him as a mature man, on the night before what he feared might be the crisis of his life. He spent the long hours wrestling, as he believed, with destiny, and would not let it go until it blessed him at the breaking of the day.

In the present age we search diligently for the causes of all things, we strive to attribute all results to the operation of definite laws, and in applying the principle to human relations we hear much of the effect of environment upon a man's career. He is the product of the time in which he lives, of the people among whom he dwells. He is a creature of suggestion, and the suggestions come from the world about him, and from the comrades with whom he associates. By the law of his being he imitates what others do; and he is constrained to win his livelihood in accord with the customs that prevail in his community. In all this there is much that is sound and of grave import; but it is also true that a man creates to a great extent his own environment. He is not affected equally by everything that surrounds him. He is mainly influenced by, and conversely his personality reacts upon, those things of which he is conscious, which he perceives. The world has many aspects, and no one sees them all. No two men see precisely the same aspect, and therefore no two men have precisely the same environment, or live in exactly the same world. Everyone perceives chiefly the things to which he pays attention, and again he pays attention to the things in which he is interested, about which he cares.

If a number of men walk through a strange country, one of them may observe the trees and plants, another the birds, a third the tracks of wild animals, a fourth the possibilities of agriculture, a fifth the roads and buildings, while a sixth may see little or nothing of any value.

Some of them may be impressed by the good qualities of the people, others by their disagreeable traits. Each of these men has virtually traveled in a different land, which is not, indeed, created by his own thoughts, but is brought to his notice thereby; and what each of them has seen goes to form his opinions and thus affects his future conduct. But if a man is moulded, if his destiny is shaped, by the world in which he lives, and if in large measure he frames that world for himself, by the nature and intensity of his own interests, it is obviously important that he should frame the right kind of world. This is not merely a question of the temperament with which he happens to have been born, for his world is made in large part by his aspirations, and by his persistence in maintaining them.

No doubt men are not in fact born either free or equal. They cannot do what they wish; their opportunities are diversely circumscribed; their natural capacities, their bodily and mental vigor, vary enormously; and yet when one has passed middle life, and looks back on the people he has known, he may well feel that the limits on freedom of action, and the inequalities of natural gifts, have been less decisive factors than he might have supposed. The differences in men's careers are often based not so much on the opportunities they have had, as upon the use they have made of them. A man is, indeed, often quite ignorant of the chances that have passed by him unobserved. We go through much of life like the young man journeying to the city to seek his fortune. In the heat of the day he lay down by the roadside and fell asleep. While he slept there two thieves, who espied him, proposed to kill and rob him, but reflecting that he was probably penniless went their way. Shortly afterwards a rich merchant passed by, and, struck by the young man's appearance, thought of offering him a position in his business; but, realizing that he knew nothing of the youth's antecedents, checked his impulse and rode on. The young man awoke and pursued his journey, unconscious that he had been close to death and to good fortune. Too often a man lets his opportunities slip away, through timidity, prejudice, or the blindness of inertia.

But after all the most important factor in shaping men's careers is commonly a difference in standards; and that means a difference in the objects for which they really care. I have a shrewd friend who has always insisted that, as a rule, men accomplish whatever they desire intensely.

Men differ amazingly in the standards they keep before their eyes. Many men seem to care chiefly for amassing wealth; others for fame or for professional success; a few for power; and some merely for ease and comfort, or even for display. I have sometimes been shocked to hear a man declare — not always I trust with perfect sincerity — that if he could accumulate a tolerable fortune by his profession or business he would retire, apparently to do nothing of any consequence. If he meant to devote himself to public service, or to those charitable institutions for the general welfare in which much of the best public work is done in our community, well and good. There is no more noble form of life, provided the motive be a desire to do good, and not a craving for power, or a passion for the acclamations of the crowd. If popular government gives to every man the privilege of serving his country, it also imposes on him the duty of doing so, as far as his circumstances will permit. Every man in

America is bound to take at least an intelligent interest in public affairs, and to bear a part of the burden of government either in office or out. He ought to perform with eagerness his duties as a citizen, and make personal sacrifices to check iniquity and promote honest, efficient administration and pure politics.

But few men are in a position to devote the greater part of their energies directly to the service of the state. Most people must perforce spend by far the larger portion of their time on their profession, business, or occupation; and their main influence upon the world for good or evil must be wrought out through, or in connection with, the effort to support themselves. Let us not, therefore, think of that influence as small or ignoble. We are altogether too much in the habit of separating life into two fractions which we regard as selfish and generous. If a man who gives liberally of his wealth and his time to beneficent objects says in his office, "Business is business, and although the Ten Commandments are followed here the Golden Rule is not," — to what extent dwelleth the love of God in him? Life is an integral whole, and by means of that which fills the greater part of it must a man's chief good in the world be done. Some years ago in a cemetery at Bologna I remember the custodian smiling contemptuously at the gravestone of a wheelwright which bore a bas-relief of a carriage spring. Probably an improvement in springs of this kind had been that man's chief contribution to the well-being of his community; and it may well have been a notable contribution. Certainly it was not a matter for ridicule that his family should record the fact over his grave; and it is perhaps unfortunate that on account of a dogmatic controversy the words, "and their works do follow them," are omitted from the burial service of the Church of England. False shame about a man's trade has not always prevailed. One of the largest ancient tombs close by the walls of Rome is that of a baker, and it displays the implements of his craft.

Let every man remember that the work he does, albeit for the immediate sake of gain, shall rise up in judgment against him. If he conducts it without regard to the rights of others, or the welfare of the public; if he needlessly crushes those weaker than he, or defrauds the ignorant who have no eyes to see, or no spokesman to defend them; then he has done a wrong which gold will not efface.

Moreover, if he has done the work that falls to his hand only fairly well, he is an unprofitable servant. He is living not, indeed, with a bad, but with a low, standard. Too many men are satisfied with mediocrity when the standard they set up for themselves should be nothing short of excellence. I think it was Lamartine who in speaking of the lifelong work of Palissy the potter said that it was like that of every profession which has labor for its means, progress for its object, and God for its end. You may recall how, in *Trilby*, Du Maurier makes the French sculptor Durien say, "I'm very much afraid He does not really exist, le bon Dieu! most unfortunately for *me*, for I *adore* Him! I never do a piece of work without thinking how nice it would be if I could only please *Him* with it." Few men achieve success worth having unless, by whatever name they call it, they are moved by a spirit of this kind. The only true standard is that of eternal perfection, and we must keep it ever before our eyes, however small in scope the work we actually do, and however feeble our capacity to approach the ideal.

If by success in life we mean attaining the goal of ambition, then success comes only to those whose standards are low; for the higher a man's standard, the more lofty his aim, the farther will he always be from reaching it. What gives life its value is not the accomplishment of something, a result that is moderately good, but the effort to do some thing as well as it can be done, and the man who strives for that will go much farther than he who fixes his gaze upon a lower point. But you will say, if a man sets his hopes beyond what he can attain, he can never be happy, because he can never have the satisfaction of reaching it. Let us not deceive ourselves. If the pursuit of happiness is one of the rights of man, it is in itself the least remunerative of occupations. Happiness is not found by hunting it, but in the course of a search for something else. It is not the aim, but a by-product, of a happy life. No scheme of philosophy can escape the eternal ethical paradox. No rational system of morality can be framed which teaches that by doing right we shall bring permanent misery upon ourselves; that the good are doomed to grief, and the bad to pleasure. Such a doctrine would shock our moral sense of justice. Every system of ethics must assume that the performance of duty brings happiness in this life or in another. And yet if the desire for happiness is the direct motive for conduct it has no moral value. A religion that is worthy of the name proclaims that it is the duty of every man to strive, in complete self-sacrifice, with all his heart, with all his soul, with all his mind, and with all his strength for the Kingdom of God — which means the working together of all things for the perfect good; and it bids him have faith that if he does so happiness will in some way come in the end.

But the means are not to be neglected for the ends. If we must keep our eyes fixed upon the stars to know our course aright, we must also look at the road we travel, lest we stumble and fall by the way. Many people who start out with bright hopes become discouraged, and after what seems a fruitless struggle give up the fight, or settle down to be content with far less than they had at first desired. Young men often expect success to come too easily. They do not realize the importance in all life's ventures of the power of work. They do not appreciate the necessity, in every career, of intense, continuous, accurate labor, and even of drudgery. Work of that kind is not only needed for headway in any pursuit; it often makes up for defects in more brilliant gifts. Among the half-truths that pass for proverbs is the saying that genius is a capacity for taking infinite pains. It is not true in the sense that great results can be wrought without imagination, but on the other hand imagination without hard work is usually barren; and what is more, the brighter the imagination the greater the amount of work required to bring its full fruition. In reading history we are amazed by a genius, a soldier it may be, or a statesman, who by one act, almost in a flash, seems to turn the current of events and achieve a lasting victory. It seems the inspiration of a moment, until by a study of details we learn with what laborious forethought, with what abundant care, he prepared the conditions that secured the best chance of a favorable issue.

Moreover, the unpremeditated act of a moment may

be the result of years of mental preparation. We admire the hero who in sudden peril at great personal risk or sacrifice does a courageous thing, and saves the lives of others. Is it a mere accident that he did so? Is it a mere chance that he found himself in a position where anyone else would have done the same? If so he deserves no special praise, for the action is no test of character, but solely the sport of fortune. It is not so, because the quick reaction of his mind is usually the consequence of long discipline of character. Deliberately or unconsciously he has schooled himself to self-restraint or noble thought, and when the emergency comes his nature responds at once to the call. If you knew him well you knew how he would act. Adventures are to the adventurous; heroic acts fall to the lot of heroes; for sudden daring is a test of quality long trained.

Young men are not only prone to underestimate the value of hard work; they are apt, also, to look for success too quickly and too certainly. Everyone with high aspirations encounters delays, disappointments, and often for a time failure; and the difference in men lies in great part in their tenacity in resisting discouragement, or in their resourcefulness in taking a fresh path when the first one has proved delusive. Destiny is mysterious, baffling; yet if pursued relentlessly may lead to success in directions unforeseen, and not designed at the outset; but it does not bless a man unless he has the endurance to wrestle with it through the darkness until the breaking of the day.

June 18, 1911

But if the watchman see the sword come, and blow not the trumpet, and the people be not warned; if the sword come, and take any person from among them, he is taken away in his iniquity; but his blood will I require at the watchman's hand.

EZEKIEL 33:6.

THE WORLD moves upward like a mountain road on a steep ascent, by zigzags. It rises by inclining first in one direction and then in another. Man progresses by over-accentuating one principle at a time; but in doing so he is apt to lose his sense of proportion, to forget that the principle in vogue at the moment does not embody the whole truth; that pursued exclusively it will not lead him to his goal; and we do well to pause at times, look about, and ascertain the direction of the distant peak.

The keynote of the present day is efficiency. We live in a material age, in which scientific advance has placed the forces of nature under man's control far more than at any preceding epoch; we are interested in visible progress, and we demand tangible results as the measure of achievement. For the contemplative sage we have little use; in mute, inglorious Miltons we wholly disbelieve. We ask of a man what he has done, and shake our heads if palpable evidence is not forthcoming. Hence our moral exhortations take the form of preaching the duty of action, unselfish action, service to the public and to suffering humanity. This is the gospel of good works. It is excellent; it is ennobling; but it is not all. Man owes to God, and to his fellow men, not only his conduct, but also his thought, not only to do much, but also to think aright, not only his acts but also his opinions.

The first subject on which a man is bound to form an opinion is the rectitude of his own conduct. Now in all the paths of active life there is a temptation not to think enough about the moral principles involved; to accept the code of ethics prevalent in the occupation to which we belong; to do what everyone else does. Business is far more easily conducted in that way, for the man who revolts against abuses instead of quietly conforming to them brings discomfort to his fellows as well as disadvantage to himself. Cogent arguments for conforming to the accepted standard are always at hand. Business, it is said, is business, not charity, and its only object is the desire of legitimate gain. It cannot be managed on the principle that the men of superior acumen ought to share with everyone else the benefits of their shrewdness. Hence they cannot be expected to show their hand. Besides, the rules of business fairness are to some extent conventional. Transactions, which everybody in the trade understands, are not fraudulent because outsiders do not comprehend their meaning. One is doing only what others do — others who are of good repute; and it is unreasonable to destroy one's prospect of success by being quixotic. Arguments like these are not wholly false. They have a proper application; but it is fatally easy to carry them to the point of justifying almost anything. Men whose principles are not of the highest believe readily that everyone acts as they do themselves, when in fact there are many people who have not so bowed the knee to Baal. They frame in their minds conventions that are not accepted by really upright men. Now if men who, without being clearly dishonest, are not very scrupulous find an advantage in a low standard, and if the better men do not distinctly and openly reject it, the standard of business integrity will have a tendency to be steadily shaved off and abased. In all such matters it is easy to be drawn downward by simple thoughtlessness without intending it, for unless serious and searching consideration is given to a question self-interest readily warps the judgment.

Moreover, to allow one's judgment to be warped by one's own interests is not the only danger. For an upright man there is a far greater temptation to allow it to be warped by the interests of others confided to his care. This has become increasingly important with the growth of combinations of capital. Almost all large concerns at the present day are corporate, so that a man of large affairs is rarely in a position to be conscientious at his own expense, and hence he feels that before repudiating a profit he must be very sure that it is improper. He is acting for other people so numerous and so scattered that he cannot consult them if he would, while they are usually interested chiefly in the dividends, and know little of the details of the business. If the scruples of the manager cause a loss of income, he may be an excellent man, highly respected, but he is unprofitable, and liable to be discarded. We suffer today from the fact that the owners of property are in large part virtually absentees, so far as its management is concerned, and that has always been a condition fraught with danger.

Observe that the things to which I refer are not gross, palpable frauds which any honest man would condemn, but practices of a questionable character which are sometimes justified, sometimes excused, and sometimes lamented as unavoidable incidents of the business. Suddenly, as in the case of railroad rebates, or illicit profits made by directors of corporations, the public becomes awakened, everyone admits the abuse, and there is an explosion which would not have occurred had the actors thought of the subject conscientiously.

Observe again that I am not urging a quixotic attitude. Every profession, every occupation, has a morality of its own, often inscrutable to the outside world, but essential to the integrity of the profession itself. The public, for example, has never been able to understand how a lawyer can properly take any case, or argue any point of law, which he does not fully believe to be right; but while a conscientious lawyer will not lend his aid to a cause that he deems fraudulent, he knows that the ends of justice are best served by having advocates urge fairly, but as strongly as they can, each side of the case, leaving the decision to an impartial tribunal. What I am urging is the duty of opinion; the duty of every man to give a careful consideration to the moral aspect of the questions arising in his occupation, and to be fully persuaded in his own mind of the rectitude of the acts he is called upon to perform.

If there is a temptation not to think, not to judge one's own conduct by high ethical standards, there is also a tendency to think loosely about all practical problems. The present age is impatient, apt to form opinions carelessly, to rush into action without taking the trouble to study a subject thoroughly. There has been, perhaps, no time in the history of the world when men have been so eager to act, and so regardless of the accuracy of the principles on which they act. No sooner is a grievance perceived than people are ready to grasp at almost any remedy proposed. This is an age of panaceas, from the quack medicine to the superficial cure-all for political and social malady. Men are not satisfied to wait until they have worked out in their minds all the consequences of a principle or line of conduct. Knowing that they are striving to cure an evil, they are full of moral enthusiasm, and feel that even if the particular remedy is unavailing the effort itself has a moral value. That is true, but again it is not the whole truth. If there were two nations, both filled with public spirit, one of them highly energetic, but wrong-headed, and constantly making blunders, the other less active, cautious, but habitually right in its solution of national problems, there could surely be no doubt that in the long run the second would endure and prosper better than the other. We are not called upon to choose between two such extreme alternatives, both qualities, of acting with energy and of thinking right, are indispensable to the national welfare, but it is the second that we are at present more in danger of neglecting.

A false principle, a false line of conduct, leads inevitably astray, and sometimes brings a revengeful Nemesis in its train. In an historical lecture one might cite lamentable examples — George Eliot, in her novels, insisted that in this world people are punished less for their sins than for their follies, or, indeed, for their mistakes; and that is not less the case of nations than of individuals. In fact the mistake is a sin in so far as it is due to a lack of care in seeking for the truth. It is a sin of mental indolence, and lies chiefly at the door of educated men.

We look with self-complacent contempt upon those who are shackled by traditional prejudices. We say that they would soon be free from those prejudices if they would open their minds and think about the matter. But surely it requires no more intellectual effort, and shows no more serious thought, to accept a superficial impression than to retain an inherited prejudice. In each case the conviction may be a true opinion based upon prolonged and careful investigation, or it may be only an assumption due to mental inertia, and if so the man who holds it is equally to blame whether the idea be old or new. He has failed in his duty to search diligently for truth and found his opinion thereon.

In a true democracy everyone is entitled to take part in forming public opinion, and since no one is exclusively charged with that duty, no one feels permanently responsible for it. We are, therefore, too prone to shunt our responsibility for holding correct opinions on public questions by casting it upon the broad shoulders of the multitude. It is for them to judge and to decide. If a mistake is made the fault is theirs, and we wash our hands in innocency. We go further, for we have a sense of protection from error by being on the popular side, the side of the majority of the whole community, or it may be of our party, our profession, our little set. There is a tendency to esteem it a virtue to shout with the biggest crowd that surrounds us, to feel that if a man is in the cheering section he not only is right, but is performing a duty which excuses him from other burdens. Men dread the obloquy of being on the unpopular side. They are oppressed by what Mr. Bryce calls the fatalism of the multitude. Those who have no faith in the doctrines of the hour lie low, waiting till the storm is passed. Surely we take the motto *Vox populi, vox Dei* too literally. It offers no discharge from personal responsibility. True religion is based on a conviction of sin, of righteousness, and of judgment; and by that is meant one's own sin, and the righteousness and judgment of God; not someone else's sin, one's own righteousness and judgment by popular vote.

I am, of course, perfectly aware that the duty of acting in every contingency in life upon a carefully formed opinion of right and wrong is not always in harmony with the most rapid success in either business or politics. Sometimes, indeed, a man may even ruin his career by adherence to his principles. A man who desires to do his duty without making any sacrifice for it is like one who seeks to be a soldier without risking his life. He may parade in a uniform in time of peace, but he is not the stuff that real soldiers are made of. Let us abandon once and for all, as a moral precept, the proverb that honesty is the best policy. In an exceptionally good environment it may be nearly true, but save within limits it is certainly not a general truth. The man who intends to live up to his principles, and has principles worth living up to, must be prepared to make no little actual sacrifice of the pleasant things of this world, and to risk the loss of much more. The man who expects to square his principles with his interests has not the root of the matter in him. He is a prudent, but not a righteous, man.

There is such a thing as truth; there is an absolute difference between right and wrong; and if we do not believe that the safety of our immortal souls depends on our success in finding it, that does not relieve us from the duty of seeking it with all the powers that we possess, nor annul the fact that the welfare of a country depends upon the success of its citizens in finding it. No doubt life is not long enough for any man to examine exhaustively every question upon which he must act. As in every other case in life we must leave aside some things we feel an obligation to do, in order that we may attend to others whose demands upon us are more imperative. Let us, however, make sure, first, that in any matter in which we are called upon to act, our failure to form an opinion based on careful study is not due to apathy, to prejudice, or to indolence; and, second, that an opinion not so formed is held tentatively and subject to revision.

Some years ago it was necessary to urge upon college men the duty of taking an active part in public affairs. They were too much inclined to hold aloof. People talked about the danger of touching pitch and being defiled; although, as Christ taught his disciples, only that which comes from within defiles a man. College men, today, are eager for service of every kind, however disagreeable it may be. The need is greater now of impressing upon them the duty of opinion than of action. Where there is no vision the people perish, or to put it in language more modern, if those who are best equipped to think deeply, and to form public opinion wisely, think loosely or advocate opinions that are inaccurate, unbalanced, and unsound, the people are in danger. An individual may win fame quickly by new and eccentric views, but for the public it is far more important that his ideas should be correct than that they should be startling. The Sphinx of destiny is ever propounding riddles for the nation to solve at its peril, and the welfare of the public depends on finding the right answer, not on devising one which is ingenious, clever, or merely suggestive.

If we believe in sin, in righteousness, and in judgment; if, in other words, we believe that there is a moral order in the world; we must feel that everything we possess we hold under an obligation to use in harmony with that moral order. There is no midway principle. Everything we have — our wealth, our natural and acquired capacities — we hold in trust to carry forward the purposes of God. If college men have nothing else, they have an education, and they ought to have acquired some capacity for thinking clearly and deeply. This faculty they possess not for merely selfish ends, but in trust to use conscientiously for the solution of the intricate problems of our political, social, and business life, and never have these problems been more difficult and more urgent than they are today.

June 16, 1912

If therefore ye have not been faithful in the unrighteous mammon, who will commit to your trust the true riches?
And if ye have not been faithful in that which is another man's, who shall give you that which is your own?
LUKE 16:11, 12.

WE LIVE in a very interesting and a very difficult age. An interesting age because the world is moving rapidly; because our command over the forces of nature, over the means of locomotion, and the transmission of knowledge, has increased at a rate hitherto unknown; and this has brought about fresh possibilities of combination, new social relations, and thereby new problems and new solutions.

An age that is interesting is also difficult, because we are not merely spectators of the human drama unrolled before our eyes. We must be actors in that drama, and play our parts, however small, at our own peril and the peril of the community in which we live. Highly civilized people cannot regard the whole duty of man as comprised in the avoidance of flagrant offenses against the moral law, and the performance of a few simple rites and family obligations. Every act, and every failure to act, has consequences; it starts a train of effects, great or small, which never ceases and can never be wholly undone, and therefore every act has a moral value. We cannot hope to be perfect in conduct, but that does not relieve us from the duty of striving to make the total good we do as large, and the total evil as little, as we can.

We look through a glass darkly; we cannot always see our path clearly; our vision is too feeble, the obstacles are too frequent, our wisdom is too slight; but to some extent we can know the direction of our way. If the world were a moral chaos, without meaning beyond selfish gratification, our existence would be like the unending warfare under the sea, where one fish can come to maturity only by ruthlessly consuming multitudes of others; where his life is preserved only by the constant sacrifice of other similar lives. But if we believe, as mankind always has believed, and by the nature of its spirit is impelled to believe, that there is a moral as well as a physical order in the world, that there are moral principles as well as natural laws, then our happiness must lie in conforming to that moral order, and it must be our duty to promote a moral harmony in the world to the utmost of our capacity.

The general principles of morality are eternal and immutable; but the means by which a moral harmony is to be attained, or rather is to be approached, vary with every age according to the state of its civilization; and in this, the age of the most complex condition that mankind has yet attained, the questions are more intricate than they were. The simpler rules of the past no longer suffice, and men are groping for means more adequate to the ends. These must be determined by the same process of reasoning that rational people apply to all the problems of life. I speak to you as educated men who have acquired some skill in verifying and marshaling facts, and in drawing inferences from them; and I want to speak about one of the difficulties that besets us at the present time, and is too apt to warp the moral judgment and dim the moral perception of well-intentioned people. It is a problem most of you will be called upon to meet, perhaps without knowing it, and all of you ought to think about it.

Everyone has heard of the evils of absentee ownership. They have become proverbial. They have been charged with being at the root of the misfortunes of the Irish tenant, and of the sufferings of the slaves in Jamaica. The fact is that absenteeism places both the owner and his steward in a false position. Neither of them acts as he would if he were both owner and manager of the estate. The owner does not see the condition of the people on his land, and the steward cannot heed it. To the absentee owner neither the estate nor the people on it are ends in themselves. They are merely a means of revenue. They are an investment, not a care, or a charge, or an occupation with its duties and responsibilities; and hence all he tends to ask is whether the revenue is as large as he has a right to expect. The steward, on the other hand, is there to collect rents or profits and to make them as large as he can. He may hear cries of distress, but what is that to him? He has no power to relieve distress. It is not his duty. He is appointed for the simple object of producing a revenue, and if he is not the man who can do that, he is not wanted, and someone who can do it will take his place.

It may seem that we have no such absentee ownership today. On the contrary, we have more of it than ever before. All our methods of co-operation, all our organized bodies, involve it to some extent. All corporations involve absentee management so far as the stockholders and managers are not identical, which can never be the case in any large concern. It is involved in all private trusts so far as the trustees are not the only beneficiaries; in all professional management of property for others; in all organizations of every kind managed by officers in the interest of other members. I am not speaking of lack of fidelity towards those whose property is confided to the managers of the corporation. The question there is only one of simple probity, of dealing as an honorable trustee would deal with his *cestuis*. He will not take advantage of his position to make a profit at their expense. The true principle is that no director of a corporation should buy or sell stock in consequence of any information which he has acquired in that fiduciary capacity, and which is not equally accessible to all the stockholders; that he should not make any incidental profit by any transaction with his corporation — such as underwriting new issues of securities — unless on the same terms that are offered to all the stockholders.

The question of what is right and what is wrong in

such cases may not always be perfectly obvious; and it may not always be perfectly easy to do one's duty; but difficulties far greater arise in the manager's relations with other people. Take such matters as injurious trades, unhealthy tenements, unfair competition with rivals, oppressive treatment of employees, dishonest products, disregard of the public safety or comfort, dealings with public authorities which, even if not corrupt, are unconscionable. It is in questions of this kind that the evils of absentee-ownership are felt today. The investor does not inquire into them, or trouble himself about them. The stock is paying large dividends and is a good investment. It may be doing business in another State, or operating all over the country, and it is not easy for him to find out what is being done. Public opinion is of little value as a guide in such things, because it is usually ill-informed and is rarely aroused until an evil has become great. In short, the moral questions involved in the management of the corporation do not thrust themselves upon the stockholder, and are rarely brought to his notice. Like the absentee landlord of an estate he thinks of the stock as an investment, and regards it primarily, if not exclusively, from the point of view of revenue; and the revenue is independent of the morality of the management. Indeed it may be greater where the management is not too scrupulous. The stockholder, therefore, is essentially in the position of the absentee landlord; and the suffering falls on the persons with whom his corporation is brought into contact — as it falls upon the tenantry or the slave gangs on an estate — not because the stockholder is malicious or hard, or personally callous, but because he is an absentee. He is not himself responsible for the management, or even aware of its problems.

The manager, on the other hand, knows that the stockholders — while very keen about the amount of their dividends — are indifferent about the manner in which they are earned. He knows that so long as the stock is profitable he is unlikely to be asked questions about the management; but that if as a result of conscientiousness in his dealings there is a fall in the dividends, he will be called to account sharply. The stockholders will say that while he is no doubt a good man, with high principles, he is not practical, lacking in business ability, and had better be replaced. Moreover, it is not merely that his interests would lead him to subordinate other questions to the size of the dividends, that this is the way to please his employers; he is led in the same direction by a sense of loyalty to the corporation that he serves. He feels a sense of duty to do the best he can for it, to fight its battles, to push its interests, and a great deal of the wrong that is done is concealed from the actors by their devotion to the welfare of the concern. Even in charitable and educational institutions one feels this strongly. They struggle against one another to the detriment of the cause in which they profess to be engaged, until the army of the Lord sometimes reminds one of that of Midian, which was destroyed before Gideon because every man's sword was against his fellow. If this be true of institutions whose professed object is unselfish, how much more of those whose primary object is gain. In such a case the manager has a sense of two distinct obligations, one to his stockholders and one to the public, and these are not infrequently more or less in conflict. For the one he will be called to account speedily by those who have power to discharge him; for the other he may be called upon to account by a vague, intangible public, which is very likely to visit his sins upon the innocent and let the guilty escape.

I remember well an upright client who said to me once that in business one could not help cracking the Golden Rule, but he tried not to break it. He was in the main managing his own property and that of his family, and he would have found it much harder to live up to his principles if he had been conducting affairs for the benefit of a multitude of stockholders with whom he never came into contact, and to whom he could, therefore, not explain his position.

The difficulty has been increased by the intense competition of modern industrial life, where the margin of profit is very small and depends upon a close scrutiny of expenditure and revenue, a scrutiny which the manager feels keenly, but the scattered owners and the public fail to comprehend. Corporations have enabled small property owners to co-operate in vast concerns, and have rolled up huge aggregations of capital, capable of increasing wealth and exerting power for good and harm on an unprecedented scale; but they have made those owners, in most cases, absentees, with all the evils of absentee-proprietorship.

These dangers can be lessened only if both owners and managers feel that property involves obligations; that it is not held for purely selfish gratification, but is affected with a trust for the community at large, to be discharged with a conscientious regard for the public welfare; that it is not merely the size of the dividends, but the service to our fellow men, for which we must give account. If we are moral beings we must assume that we hold property, and every other power that we possess, to promote moral ends; that it is not enough to comply with the low standard that the fashion of the day demands, but that unless we do our duty to the utmost we are unprofitable servants. A keen French observer remarked that he had heard of America as the land of the almighty dollar, but on visiting it he found that wealth was valued here for reasons different from those that prevailed in Europe. There it was regarded as cash to be spent for pleasure. Here it was prized for the power it conferred. Power to do what? To do good or harm? To magnify the possessor and crush obstacles to his will, or to promote the progress of the people? That is the question on which the destiny of our nation hangs.

Most college graduates own or manage property to some extent — to a far greater extent than the average of the community — and those who do not are sometimes singularly ignorant about it. Therefore it is important for them to think clearly upon these subjects. For good or for evil our social system is based upon the private ownership of property; but property involves duties as well as privileges, and it is on the proper discharge of these that the ownership is morally if not practically conditioned. The first duty of the owner of property is to manage it himself so far as he can. So far as he cannot, it is his duty to see that it is managed as he ought to manage it himself; and a man who manages the property of others ought to do so with as large a sense of moral obligation as if it were his own. This may seem a paradox, but it is not. The temptation to be selfish for one's own profit is stronger, but for a good man it is easier to resist, than the temptation to be selfish in acting for the benefit of others. I am not speaking to bad men, to dishonest men, or men of hard selfishness; but to honest, upright, and large-hearted men, who mean to do their duty in their day and generation. To such a man life consists not in the multitude of things that he possesses, but in the use that he makes of them.

If to a band of young men going abroad to do God's work in the world it seems strange to speak on such a sordid theme as the care of property, let it be remembered that the social relations brought about by the new forms of property lie at the basis of most of the intricate problems of our modern life, and that the straight path to a righteous solution of those problems lies in a sense of duty on the part of the possessor. It is the habit of the day to decry loudly the iniquity of others, to assume that in attacking them we perform our public duty; that by reforming them we fulfill the moral law. Such an attitude has its value. It corrects gross abuses; but by itself it is not a principle that makes for the highest type of civilization. Carlyle remarked of the French Revolution that everyone wanted to reform the world, but no one began by reforming himself. Great moral improvements come from a conviction of moral obligation rather than from outside forces stimulated by selfish motives. Let no one think that he can manage property rightly with the utmost benefit to himself, or the last farthing of immediate profit to his fiduciaries. Let him not try to square his obligations wholly with his interests. Duty in every relation in life involves some sacrifice, or it would have no moral significance. It would be nothing but a highly intelligent selfishness. If you are not prepared for sacrifice you are not in harmony with a moral order in the world. If you are not faithful in the unrighteous mammon, who will commit to your trust the true riches? If you have not been faithful in that which is another man's, who shall give you that which is your own?

June 15, 1913

> And when Saul saw David go forth against the Philistine, he said unto Abner, the captain of the host, Abner, whose son is this youth? And Abner said, As thy soul liveth, O king, I cannot tell.   I SAMUEL 17:55.

THIS was a fatal moment in the history of Israel, the nation which was bound to influence more deeply than any other the religious opinion of modern Europe, which was in sore stress, and, in fact, in danger of extinction.

Until David appeared to go out against Goliath nobody else dared to, and it looked as though their armies would be hopelessly defeated and driven back. Just then there appeared this young shepherd. Now, David had three qualifications for going forth against Goliath. One of them was that he had the heroism to expose himself to what was believed to be absolutely certain death, and, secondly, he had the faith that he would succeed, and the third quality that he had was the good sense, the intelligence, the wisdom — call it what you please — in short, the imagination to understand that there was no use to oppose a giant by brute force, and that his only chance lay in the use of a missile.

Without going into the question of predestination we may fairly say that Christianity is ruled entirely by faith. It requires men having authority in the government of the world, so as to make it possible for man to help and not hinder the plan of God. Men can regulate the future of mankind on this plan. But if we do not believe in fatalism imposed on mankind as a whole, we are, nevertheless, in very serious danger of falling into a belief of another kind — the fatalism which may be called the fatalism of the multitude. We are a little too much inclined to think that the individual is carried along by the spirit of his age, and that he has all he can do to go along with that spirit.

Now, that is not true. Men are not necessarily sheep. Men do not have to behave like sheep. James Russell Lowell in the later years of his life remarked that he had seen many spirits of the age and some of them never came on as expected, and that is unquestionably true. It is very much in the hands of any man, who chooses to do so, to have a very perceptible influence on the spirit of the age in which he lives and on the destiny of the age which is to follow. There has never been any time in the history of the world when the opportunity for the individual man has been so great as it is in the years that lie immediately before us today. The world is more plastic than it has ever been before; the world is less held by its fixed traditions. It is more ready to adopt new ideas: it is more ready to turn into new paths. It is less content with the conditions it has reached, the results already achieved, than it has been in any period of history. The world is ready to follow.

I have said nothing, as you observe, as yet of politics,

because in this country politics can hardly be said to be a profession in a desirable sense. Nevertheless, politics is the business of every man. If democracy means the right of everyone to take an interest and a part in public affairs, it means, also, that he should do so. In the past, democracy meant the opportunity of every man to put forth his utmost effort. Now, in politics, we need you more than we ever needed those before you. What we need, however, is not a larger number of itinerant vendors of patent remedies. What we need is men who will make a scientific diagnosis of the disease from which the public suffers. We want to have men who will think out the questions which we shall encounter — who will think them out scientifically and earnestly — who will face them fearlessly; because, remember this, the rare men who have stood in the forefront of the advance of civilization have not usually found themselves shouting with the largest crowd. We require, above all, courage, and the courage we require is not only the courage of action; it is the courage of thought, the courage of thinking right. If the men in the country who want to do right would think right, our doing right would follow almost as a matter of course.

Now, to return to my text for a moment. In days like those of Saul and Israel, it was almost impossible for a young man without family, without wealth, without standing in the community, to go forth as a leader. But it is an everyday fact today that any man can go forth as a leader, if he has qualities which make him fit to do it.

Now, let us note this one thing. Just as in David's case the victory today is not necessarily to the strong. David, as I have said, had the wit to see that there was no use facing a giant by brute force. He could bring no brute force to compare with that of the giant. It was the intelligent use of the means which lay within his reach that enabled him to win.

We are to accomplish results in the world by knowing how to do it, and, therefore, it is that we speak with more confidence to educated men. It is the educated man to whom we must look forward to solve the problems that are crowding upon us.

Moreover, let me point out to you another thing. The achievement is not only for those who are abnormally gifted.

William James, I remember when I was in college, pointed out to me how many young men there were who never succeeded in accomplishing anything. He said, "Ability is very well, but many men of ability fall by the wayside and never reach any particular goal for lack of enterprise, lack of industry, lack of those things which we sum up under the general heading of force of character." And William James was in the habit of saying to his classes, and elsewhere, that any man who would devote his whole strength for a sufficient number of years to mastering any subject would wake up some day to find he was an authority on that subject, and an authority means a leader in thought. Any man who has the force of character can accomplish much. But without force of character, which means earnestness, determination, persistence, and industry, talent is of little value, and any man who has those moral qualities will accomplish more than he or his friends ever dreamed was within his reach.

Now, let me point out one other thing to you, and

that is what we mean by accomplishing something. Are you thinking of reputation? If your idea is reputation, you will get your reward. Reputation is a fairly easy thing to get. A little judicious advertising and a little putting forth of one's self will bring a great deal of reputation. Reward is not necessarily of real value to a man who has a deep, earnest conviction of what he wants to do in life. It is the act which is the life itself, and not the fame of it that is precious. If the life is what your object is, remember that any man with force of character who will make himself the master of anything by persistence and by energy can do the act and live the life which will tell, whether the world outside ever knows it or not. And he can do it more than ever before because the world is in a plastic state where anybody can put it in his hand and build the mould.

I can remember very well the people of the past generation — the generation which is now going off the stage — I can remember their point of view, and I remember what they thought about a man's making himself a marked man. If he chose to have an influence upon the current events of the world, if he chose to be a man who was at the helm, he might well do it; but one was under no obligation to do it.

It seems to me that our view of life in that respect has changed, that we recognize that wherever there is an opportunity there is a duty. We recognize that if David could kill Goliath it was his duty to do so. We recognize that David would not only not have been a hero, but he would have been a sinner, if he simply sat down and said, "I am content, let him who wants to go forward attack Goliath." I cannot myself conceive how any man with a heart in him can see the battle of the world going on before his face and not take an active part in it.

Those of us who are past middle life look to the young men in whose training we are proud to have had a share, to help the world forward on its way, and we look to them with confidence.

June 14, 1914

> *Now Elisha was fallen sick of his sickness whereof he died. And Joash the king of Israel came down unto him, and wept over his face, and said, O my father, my father, the chariot of Israel, and the horsemen thereof.*
>
> *And Elisha said unto him, Take bow and arrows. And he took unto him bow and arrows.*
>
> *And he said to the king of Israel, Put thine hand upon the bow. And he put his hand upon it: and Elisha put his hands upon the king's hands.*
>
> *And he said, Open the window eastward. And he opened it. Then Elisha said, Shoot. And he shot. And he said, The arrow of the Lord's deliverance, and the arrow of deliverance from Syria: for thou shalt smite the Syrians in Aphek, till thou have consumed them.*
>
> *And he said, Take the arrows. And he took them. And he said unto the king of Israel, Smite upon the ground. And he smote thrice, and stayed.*
>
> *And the man of God was wroth with him, and said, Thou shouldest have smitten five or six times: then hadst thou smitten Syria till thou hadst consumed it: whereas now thou shalt smite Syria but thrice.*   II KINGS 13:14–19.

THIS is the story of the visit of the young king to the dying prophet, to seek his advice, or merely to pay his tribute of respect. No doubt Joash was well intentioned or he would not have come; but we may suppose that the prophet thought he perceived a weakness in his character, or in the working of the spirit of God through him, which to Elisha was probably much the same thing. In the striking of the ground thrice only, he seemed to detect a lack of the persistence sorely needed by the ruler of the kingdom in those troubled times, and therefore he was wroth. But whatever it was that moved Elisha so strongly, this story, like many of those in the Old Testament, is built on simple human qualities, and hence contains a truth of wider application. An older man speaking to young men looks forward and backward.

The men who make a rapid success in their first venture in life are not numerous, and some of them are actually injured if they do. A young man must perforce choose his career before he has tried it. He must estimate his own qualities, with which he is still only partly familiar; and he must guess how well they fit him for an occupation of which he has had no personal experience. He judges of a profession, for example, by its intellectual side. His turn of mind may be so analytical and logical that he feels rightly a fitness for the study of law; or he has a taste for the biological sciences which attracts him to medicine; but he may or may not lack the enterprise, tact, and skill that bring clients and patients. It is no wonder then that he sometimes makes a mistake, or finds the road harder and longer than he expected. Among the men I happen to have known, few have made a quick success — and their marked success — in the thing they first undertook. Some have become disheartened and given up the fight. Almost all have gone through periods of discouragement, some to win a victory in the career first chosen, others to win it in quite a different one. The successful men have smitten, not once, or thrice, but until success came, and then have kept on smiting.

Success is, no doubt, an illusive thing, very hard to measure, and it is still more difficult to mark the steps on the way thereto. Let no man, therefore, be discouraged by failure to achieve an early success in the eyes of men. The world usually — not invariably, but usually — judges a man's product justly enough; but much time often passes before the world has a chance to judge it, and until that time comes a man must measure himself, not by what the world thinks he could do, but by the progress of his own command of the tools of his trade. Success in the long run is founded mainly on the mastery of a subject, on comprehensiveness and accuracy in dealing with its problems; and in most pursuits such a mastery requires long years, sometimes the better part of a lifetime. This does not mean that there is any time to spare; that there is no need of hastening along the road. A working life is short enough at the best, a span in which each year is the father of the next and determines the heritage of all that follow. But it is a reason for not being discouraged by lack of early recognition. If a man has an unusual mastery of any subject, if he can do something better than others can do it, the chances are that in time he will have a good market for his wares.

As one travels along the road of life, the perspective changes. Things that appeared high sink lower in the landscape, while other things bulk larger than they did at first. The towers in the town are less conspicuous, and the long low hill behind it, that hardly seemed an eminence, stands well above them and covers the horizon. So as one reviews the careers of many men, one's estimate of the value of different qualities undergoes a change. One sees what comparatively small results are accomplished by ability and intellectual brilliancy alone, unconnected with the moral qualities of earnestness in purpose, of industry, and of persistence. We call these qualities moral, not because they are by any means always directed to moral ends, but to distinguish them from pure intellectual capacity. They are moral in the sense that they are related to character, and determine the force and steadiness with which an object is pursued, be that object in itself good or bad. They are the qualities most important in the attainment of that object. At the bar, in medicine, in science, in politics, in business, in almost every career, men of moderate capacity, without striking originality, but possessed of good sense and adequate equipment for their tasks, have achieved very much by hard work, long sustained; while many a man of high talent has accomplished little or nothing worth doing, from a lack of incentive or of perseverance. To reach the very highest results both qualities are essential. Such a combination is, of course, rare; but the moral qualities are indispensable for any considerable achievement. Moreover, we must remember that natural gifts come to us mainly at birth from causes beyond our power, while the moral qualities, although in great part innate, can be cultivated to an almost indefinite extent, and are therefore subject to our own control.

A very notable fact about these moral qualities is that they are wholly transferable from one career to another. A knowledge of law, for example, is of trifling importance in most other occupations, but earnestness, industry, and perseverance, acquired in the study and practice of law, are of just as much value in any other field as if they had been acquired therein. The same thing is true of the same qualities wherever acquired. They are the strong foundations on which all success is built; and to an extent sometimes unseen, and usually unforeseen, they determine what the structure shall be. Superstitious people in all ages have regarded destiny as a mysterious power independent of us, which controls our future, lies in wait for us when we least suspect it, and dogs our steps. It does, in fact, dog our steps, precedes or follows us, clings to us, may please or provoke us, sadden us, scare us, or haunt us. We cannot shake it off nor flee away from it, any more than we can from our own shadow, but like our shadow, it is not independent of us. The shade you cast upon the ground as you walk is the shadow of your body, and the destiny that goes with you is the shadow of your mind and character. There are, of course, grave differences of opportunity among men, and they count for much. It would be absurd to pretend not to see them, or to make light of them. But it is also a mistake to throw upon them the blame for our own shortcomings. In this twentieth century America of ours the difference in men's success — not the difference in wealth, but in the achievement of things that are really worth doing — that difference, is due less to opportunities presented than to taking full advantage of those that come.

If success in life depends largely upon the moral qualities to which I have referred, and if those qualities are under our own control, it is obviously of vital importance to ask how they can be cultivated. The answer is so commonplace that it seems hardly worth making. Like all moral qualities they are developed by use — and by use alone. The man who indulges himself will become self-indulgent. The man who schools himself to subordinate his immediate desires to a distant object will become earnest and persevering; and as a part thereof, if he works steadily and hard when he does not want to do so, he will become industrious. To some men this comes easier than to others, and the man with the least appetite for work has to work the hardest to form the habit of work. Unfortunately, this is true of many things in life. It is the penalty paid by the individual for the benefit to the whole from variety of temperament.

I have said that success is an illusive thing, very hard to measure, and sometimes a man does not himself know whether he has made a success or not. One of the merchants in Boston, in the middle of the last century, conceived the brilliant idea of sending ice to India. To keep it from melting in the long voyage of a sailing ship through tropical seas was no easy matter, and ship after ship came back with the tale that the ice was all gone when she reached Calcutta. One of the captains reported that the voyage had again been a failure, for when the hold was opened there was not, he said, a piece of ice in it bigger than a man's head. Mr. Tudor asked him whether there was really so large a piece of ice as that, and making sure of it, exclaimed that success was won, feeling confident that if the water in the hold had been kept nearly at the freezing point, a little more skill would save the bulk of the cargo; and so it proved. Life is often a long series of failures which add up to a notable success. Some of the leaders in political reforms, in human thought, in religion, some of the world's greatest benefactors, have gone to their graves believing that they had made failures, when in fact they had planted the seed which no force could stop from bearing fruit in its season. They had not the patience and faith of Kepler who said of his book on astronomy that it might well wait a hundred years for a reader, as God had waited thousands for an observer. Every martyr for any cause has been, if not in his own eyes, at least in those of the multitude, a failure.

Success is certainly an elusive thing. Does it mean the mere satisfaction of desires or ambitions, whatever they may be? If a man's desire is to gratify immediate cravings for pleasure with as little exertion as possible, and he does so, has he made a success of his life? Clearly not. The mere satisfaction of desire, then, is not success unless the object desired is worthy. Is a man successful if he attains the object, worthy enough perhaps, for which he set forth in early life; and unsuccessful if he fails to attain it, although he does accomplish something else which gratifies him far less, but is of more value to others? Is real success to be measured by the extent to which the object sought has been reached, or by the intrinsic worth of the result achieved?

If success is to be measured by the attainment of the objects for which men set out on the ventures of life, then there are very few successes in the world; and those mostly of a rather poor quality. Unless a man has a peculiarly contented disposition, or ambitions not of an exalted kind, he is rarely satisfied with his achievements; and the higher his goal, the farther he will, no doubt, usually go, but the farther he will probably be from reaching it. True success does not depend upon achieving the objects a man has set before himself at the outset of his career, on the satisfaction of ambitions, or aims, or on being contented with what he has attained. Happiness and contentment depend upon the relation between desires and the ability to satisfy them, or to think one has satisfied them. A clam is happy at high water, if it needs nothing but high water to make it happy; but a higher organism requires more, and commonly more than it gets. Discontent does not signify either moral excellence or defective character. It may go with either. Some of the saints and heroes have been highly self-satisfied, and others have been deeply distressed by their own imperfections; some have gone through periods of both exaltation and depression.

True success does not consist in doing what we set forth to do, what we had hoped to do; not even in doing what we have struggled to do; but in doing something that is worth doing. One of the Rabbinic "Sayings of the Fathers" declared, "It is not thy duty to complete the work, but neither art thou free to desist from it." There are hosts of men who have never had the satisfaction of succeeding in what they have undertaken, who have been to all appearances failures, and to whom omniscience can say "Well done, good and faithful servants." The gratification even of the most laudable aims, ambitions, and desires is not the object of life. That object lies beyond our personal satisfaction, contentment, or happiness; and it is the very fact that it does so, which makes the life of a man worth living. We may explain to ourselves this paradox in different ways, according to the nature of our philosophy; and some explanation of it lies at the root of all religion. The man who, in fact, directs his life on the principle that it has no object beyond his own gratification, is not worthy of respect, because he has not risen to the moral stature of a man; and one who, without an intelligent conviction, lives for and outside himself, works by a rule of thumb, instead of the light of reason. The man who sees clearly how and why the object of his life lies outside of and beyond himself, and to whom the solution of the problem has become a deep conviction in the innermost recesses of his soul, has the greatest sustaining power this world affords.

June 20, 1915

The light of the body is the eye: if therefore thine eye be single, thy whole body shall be full of light.
MATTHEW 6:22.

THE COURSE of a man's growth and decline is a rapid increase of size and power, physical and mental, until maturity; and then something very near a level, followed by a slow and gradual falling away.

The maxima of physical and mental power do not come at the same age, but they are not very far apart. Loss of capacity to hear the highest notes is said to come at twenty-three. William James used to say that one rarely, if ever, learned a new subject after twenty-nine. Singularly true is this of work of pure imagination. Coleridge at that age had written Christabel, Kubla Khan, and the Ancient Mariner. As life goes on later knowledge grows, experience is gained, judgment becomes more balanced; but pure mental capacity is not enlarged.

You are about at the physical, and not very far from the mental, zenith of your natural powers. Rarely do men make, and therefore as a rule you have not made, the most of the opportunities of college; and probably those who have come nearest to doing it realize this best. The rest of life is still before you. Are you going to make the most of it?

I cannot understand how anyone can be satisfied to do the minimum required to get through life respectably; how without moving hand or foot to help he can stand aside as an idle spectator while the struggle and the work and the suffering of the world passes before his gaze; how he can enjoy his own little pleasures, groan over his little griefs, and take no part — not even a small one — in the great drama of life. Such a man is at best harmless and insignificant. Of such Dante said, *Non ragioniam di lor, ma guarda e passa*: Let us not talk about them, but take a look at them and pass on. Yet mere energy, enthusiasm, and activity are not enough. These qualities are necessary; they are the warp of the fabric of life, but unguided by intelligence they are not sufficient. A squirrel whirling in a rotary cage has these qualities in abundance, but to no profit. Some years ago a woodpecker displayed them all for a long time by rapping at the copper gutter of Emerson Hall. He made much noise and attracted no little attention, but his labor was not useful. Something more than energy is needed for a man's work.

I shall speak only of one quality among those that are essential for any high degree of usefulness, and that is the ability to judge oneself.

An inmate of an insane asylum although completely unconscious of his own mental condition is often perfectly aware of the state of mind of his companions. We hear tales of one patient referring to another as clearly out of his head, for the poor fellow thinks himself Napoleon, which is absurd because the speaker himself is really Napoleon. Now insanity is largely a matter of degree. How often do we hear a man assert that someone else with whom he disagrees is bitterly prejudiced, when his reason for thinking so is that the other man differs from the speaker who is firmly convinced that his own opinion is founded not at all on prejudice, but on the clear light of truth which must appeal to any impartial mind. The reasoning is precisely that of the lunatic who thought himself Napoleon. Often in such cases the men are like the two knights who fell to blows in disputing about the color of a shield, each having seen only one side of it when the two sides were of different colors. If one of those knights killed the other he committed an unpardonable murder, because he had the means of knowing that the quarrel was baseless and failed to use them. He acted before thinking enough, and he thought wrong. "Be sure you are right and then go ahead" is an excellent motto, provided it does not mean, as is frequently the case, "Shut your mind to all restraining influences and then go blindly forward."

Of course everyone realizes that there is a danger on the opposite side, a danger that resolution and enthusiasm will fade, by being sicklied o'er by the pale cast of thought. Some men are by nature lacking in decision. They cannot balance the various arguments for or against a question. These all appear of equal weight, and the scales of the mind do not register a definite result; or they move up and down with each new suggestion.

There comes a time in human affairs when a balance must be struck and opinions form the basis of conduct, or action will fail altogether.

This is a danger to be guarded against; but in our age of rapid movement, when one stimulus crowds upon another in a ceaseless flow, it is not so great a temptation as the formation of opinion on partial knowledge, and insufficient sympathy with other men's point of view. The extremist, the advocate of a panacea, the man who has only one idea and urges it with a narrow fanaticism, often accomplishes much: and if measurably successful wins loud applause. But the same fervor coupled with broader sympathy and sound judgment accomplishes much more.

There is no greater responsibility in life than the responsibility for opinion, because opinion is the basis of conduct and determines what a man does and what he is; also because it is contagious and determines his influence in the world for good or evil — out of opinions are the issues of life. We send you forth from this place to form your own judgments in the world. The college has made, and ought to make, no attempt to equip you with a complement of opinions, passed out from the professor's chair ready made and guaranteed correct. If you have learned anything worth while you have learned now to form opinions of your own. You have been taught not so much truth as the way to discover truth. That teaching you must use with what skill you may at your own peril and the peril of the community in which you live — use it under a deep sense of responsibility, and see to it that your opinions are real, serious, capable of providing a basis for action; and see that your conduct conforms to the opinions that you hold.

Above all do not deceive yourself by letting your interest, or your conduct, form your opinions. Be honest with yourself. It is bad enough to deceive another, but to deceive oneself is to be a fool as well as a knave. If you do wrong, if you fail to carry out your good resolutions fully, do not make excuses to yourself for yourself. Do not tell yourself that you were hardly placed, that there was some justification for you under the circumstances, or that everybody else does the same — which by the way is never true, although it may usually be made to appear true, if you take into account only those who do the things you are seeking to excuse in yourself. In short, do not change your opinions or your standard, because you find it hard to live up to the opinions or standard you have formed. It is less comfortable, but wiser and more moral, to admit yourself a sinner than to make your moral standards fit your besetting sin.

Change your opinions, of course; the man who never changes them is incapable of new ideas. Change them if you must, because your experience shows that they are impracticable or utopian, in other words, because you find that they are true only in part: but do not change them because they are uncomfortable for you personally. Change them because you are convinced they are wrong, not because you find it hard to live up to them. Moreover, be sure in your own mind that you have changed them. Never compromise with yourself by losing some faith in your convictions, and giving yourself in your conduct the benefit of the doubt. Avoid, as you would avoid pestilence, the danger of slowly letting down your standard of life, by constantly yielding and condoning, until the standard has lost its compelling force. If your earlier ideals seem to become not wholly true, frame another system, having in view what you think your best neighbor, or your ideal man, would be; and if you cannot live up to it, acknowledge your shortcomings without blurring your ideal. While the eye remains single the body has light and the way is clear, although one may be unable to follow it: but if the eye is dimmed the path is lost. Youth is the time of aspiration and ideals, the later course of life tries men by the standards they have already formed.

The essential defect in our life is that we do not look upon ourselves from a high enough plane, but from our own low level. Among the many tales related of Lincoln — who is rapidly becoming for the benefit of his people, in some respects a legendary character — there are few more impressive than that of his interview with the clergymen who asked him if it was not a comfort to think that in this time of stress the Lord was on our side. To their surprise and dismay Lincoln replied that he was not thinking much about that; and added, "What I want to be sure of is that we are on the Lord's side." *

If we could see ourselves, the things about us and our relation to them, as God sees them, we should lack neither correct opinions nor force of will to act upon them; and the nearest approach we can make to that is to try to place ourselves at the standpoint of a being in-

---

* This reference to Lincoln appears again — years later. Only two or three such repetitions have been found and all have been retained. All are significant. For instance, Lowell came of a group which supported Bell and Everett; but as the years passed he was more and more impressed by Lincoln's moral qualities. He was always addressing a new audience at the busiest time of his year. There is no evidence that he ever reread a sermon.

finite in knowledge, in aspiration, and in compassion. Then we shall be as nearly God-like as imperfect creatures can be.

June 18, 1916

> ... *fire shall try every man's work of what sort it is.*
> *If any man's work abide which he hath built thereupon, he shall receive a reward.*
> *If any man's work shall be burned, he shall suffer loss: but he himself shall be saved; yet so as by fire.*
> I CORINTHIANS 3:13–15.

THERE is a great difference between excellence of intentions and the value of work done. We are prone to judge strangers by what they have done; but our friends, and especially ourselves, by intentions. To some extent we are right in so doing because we judge ourselves and our friends from the standpoint of personal uprightness and morality, while we often judge men we know only by reputation on the basis of an external standard of civic achievement and public service.

But it is not only by what men have actually accomplished that we judge them; we are often influenced in our estimate of their character by the opinions they profess. This also is neither unnatural nor wholly devoid of good sense. In reading St. Paul's epistles one is constantly struck by the frequency of his moral censure of men with whose opinions he does not agree. No doubt some of his opponents taught immoral doctrines; but it must be remembered also that St. Paul was by temperament a statesman. He was striving to build a church on principles that would insure cohesion and resist the forces that must certainly attack it in the vast cosmopolitan life of the Roman Empire. He saw clearly the extreme importance of holding fast to correct opinions in the infancy of the religious body he was engaged in moulding.

From the standpoint of civilization, of the collective conscience, of social progress, opinion is a factor of momentous consequence. It is the foundation on which the whole social fabric rests, and hence the responsibility of men for their opinions is very great. It is the opinion of individuals that has condemned polygamy, slavery, cruelty to children, and cruelty to animals. In a democracy we are sometimes tempted to forget this; we are disposed to run with the crowd, cast the responsibility for the result on the broad shoulders of the public, and go our way rejoicing or complaining. If one were a despot he would often have reason to repent in sackcloth and ashes for mistakes he had innocently made; while, if he is only one of thousands who have erred, he solaces himself by saying that the people blundered. How many men are really grieved, and blame themselves seriously, when convinced that they voted wrongly at the last election? We see our responsibility for being right or wrong far more clearly in private life, especially when the welfare of others is dependent upon us. George Eliot in her novels worked out the principle that people in this world suffer quite as much for their stupidity, and their blunders, as for their sins, and others suffer with them. This principle holds both in individuals and in communities. In a moral aspect it is true that every man's work is tried by fire. If it is not sound and true it will be destroyed, although he may himself be saved by the rectitude of his intentions.

Personal righteousness and right opinions are, however, by no means the same thing, and should not be confused. Let us insist upon the inexorable responsibility for opinion. Let us be certain that we have done all we can to insure that our own opinion is correct, and then let us express it and act upon it with courage and without flinching. Let us fight for it with all our power; but let us not therefore think meanly of the character of him who conscientiously disagrees with us. Let us condemn wickedness boldly; but let us not attribute wrong motives to honorable opponents; and conversely let us never use as an argument against a principle the personal fault or moral weakness of him who argues for it. The *argumentum ad hominem*, the attempt to discredit an opinion by casting aspersions on the person who holds it, is as unjust as it is unreasonable, as immoral as it is illogical. In the long run it is true that evil communications corrupt good manners, or, in more modern language, wrong principles lower the moral standards of mankind; but it is by no means true that a man who honestly holds an erroneous opinion is a bad man, or that the opinions of a bad man are presumptively wrong.

The riddle of human life which all religions have sought to solve in different ways is the existence of evil. Grief comes from physical causes and from sin; but the sufferings of men have flowed quite as much from differences of opinion crystallized into conflicting customs, traditions, laws, beliefs, and standards of life, as from conscious wickedness or breach of the moral code of the community. Wars and quarrels come, indeed, in part from lust; but they are maintained also out of a good conscience striving for the right as it sees the right, but led by a collective prejudice.

When Samuel told Saul that the Lord had cast him away because he had spared the lives of prisoners taken in war; when he hewed the captive King Agag in pieces with a sword, he was not guilty in his own eyes of wicked cruelty. He was carrying out what he believed to be the Lord's will. He was on the Lord's side, fighting his battles; for his master was the God of Israel, and cared nothing for their foes. The Philistines had their gods also, who were the enemies of Jehovah; and so long as the supernatural powers were tribal gods the theory was rational. But when men believe in one God, who is the Father of all, their sentiments toward their opponents ought to be different; and yet men still love their friends and hate their enemies. The sentiment lies deep in human nature. Most men tend to think less well of people with whom they are in controversy over a matter of opinion — not to speak of cases of divergent interests — and when large groups of men disagree, collective dislike or co-operative selfishness is apt to assume the aspect of a virtue.

Under the greatest stress even deliberate injuring of opponents appears positively meritorious. Look at the men in the hosts fighting on land and sea in Europe today. They are striving to kill each other. Are they doing wrong? Some men who brought on the war intentionally, or by a blunder, may have done very wrong. It is not our business in this house to judge them; but the young men who fill the armies on both sides are doing their plain duty. Can anyone think they would do right on either side to throw down their arms and run away? Whatever the cause for which they fight, for them it is a call to the last full measure of devotion, to a duty they must fulfill; and in heroic spirit millions of them are going to the sacrifice.

There is a pathos in all human life, but none other so deep as this of gallant young men throwing away their lives, or the members without which life is worse than a burden, in order to kill and cripple other men for reasons that they do not and cannot understand. Their own sufferings, and those of the families they leave behind, are appalling. Yet there is no use in sighing in impotent sentimentality. With human nature as it exists, and with the world organized as it is today, these things will happen, and may happen to us hereafter.

That they are out of harmony with the spirit of our religion and civilization no one will deny; and yet they are merely a manifestation in an intense form of a tendency to be found constantly in the relations between men, or groups of men, in civil life. Every agitator, every controversialist, every leader of men, knows that one of the most powerful instruments for binding his followers together, and arousing their enthusiasm, is to provoke their moral indignation against their opponents. It is an effective and deadly weapon, which men are under a strong temptation to use, and which the unreflecting mass receives from them with a sense of complacent virtue. I remember a time when some good people seemed to think it a sign of loyalty to their alma mater to judge harshly, think meanly, and speak disparagingly of another college.

People often feel that in great national crises, in the blazing ordeal of war, it is essential and quite right to rouse men to the highest pitch of enthusiasm by inflaming their passions against the enemy. But while the struggle of the Civil War was still hot, when the end was not yet fully in sight, Lincoln in his second inaugural address spoke of the two parties to the conflict in language that will never be forgotten. "Both read the same Bible and pray to the same God, and each invokes His aid against the other. It may seem strange that any men should dare to ask a just God's assistance in wringing their bread from the sweat of other men's faces, but let us judge not, that we be not judged. . . . With malice toward none, with charity for all, with firmness in the right as God gives us to see the right, let us finish the work we are in, to bind up the nation's wounds . . . and cherish a lasting peace among ourselves and with all nations." Who shall say how much these sentiments and words of Lincoln helped the final reconciliation between North and South? We may be sure that they would have hastened the return of good feeling if he had not been slain.

We cannot work a sudden change in human nature, or bring the millennium by dreaming of it. But each new generation has a chance to make the world a little better by reducing the force of passions and motives, of habits of thought and feeling, that tend to evil. It has been remarked that the moral progress of mankind in civilization has been based upon bringing under control one after another of the primordial instincts or passions of human nature; and, if each new generation has a chance to make an advance in this direction, where shall we look for that advance, if not to those who have had the highest education among moral surroundings. They can at least make the spirit of a higher civilization and of true religion prevail more fully so far as their personal influence extends. They can cultivate the habit, in all relations in life, of not permitting differences of opinion, of interest, of class, or of environment, to blind them to the virtues of honorable opponents, or to stifle kindly feelings and mutual respect; and this can be done without blunting the purpose to make that which they believe just and wise prevail, or lessening their aversion to moral faults.

It would, indeed, be lamentable, and betoken a backward step in civilization, if we could not draw moral lessons, as well as military ones, from this war; lessons of charity, fair dealing, and mutual understanding. Quite apart from international relations, the war will in all probability be followed by social problems, insistent and difficult in the highest degree. This will be true not only of the belligerent nations, but in our own country as well; and the question whether they shall be met in a mutual spirit of fairness, justice, and good feeling, or with an acrimonious and exasperating temper, will have a serious, perhaps a permanent, effect upon the future of mankind. In that issue young men, and above all educated young men, will play, as they always must play, an important part. It is in this spirit that the college sends her sons forth into the world to fight the battle of life for righteousness, for justice, and for good will toward men.

June 17, 1917

And let it be, when thou hearest the sound of a going in the tops of the mulberry trees, that then thou shalt bestir thyself: for then shall the Lord go out before thee.

II SAMUEL 5:24.

THE BUGLE has sounded and our youth is girding on its armor. The call affects men in three different ways. There are those who could go to the battle, but, unless compelled, will not; those who want to go but cannot; and those who both can and will go. In the community at large there are many of the first of those classes. Many of these men have families; many of them will volunteer later. I have nothing to say to them here, for they are few among our students. The men who graduate this week belong almost wholly to the other two categories — those who have gone, or are fitting themselves to go, to the war; and those who are incapacitated for military service.

To those who are going forth to war it is unnecessary to speak of courage, of constancy, of fidelity, or of humanity to the wounded or captured enemy; but there are other matters on which a word of advice may not be out of place.

Under instructors particularly qualified to teach the art of present-day warfare you are being trained in the duties of officers, and those of you who possess the natural aptitude are certain — be it earlier or later — to attain the position which your abilities and proficiency deserve. Learn all you can about the profession on which you are for the time entering. In any command, the success or failure of the duty assigned you, the lives of the men under you, may depend upon the care with which you have made your preparations, or upon your readiness to act rightly in a sudden situation, a readiness that is born of thinking much beforehand. Study also to be fully competent for a grade above the one that you may hold. A fragment of flying shell, a chance bullet from a machine gun, may take away your superior, and cast his responsibility on you.

Not the lives and efficiency only of the soldiers depend upon their officers, but also in large measure their morale and their morality. Let no man despise thy youth, but be in character older than your men. See that they have reason to respect your knowledge of your work, your diligence, integrity, justice, and self-control, and the care that you take of their safety and comfort. Share with them everything that you can properly share, their ardor, their privations, everything but their misgivings. Be loyal, not in act alone, but in thought, to your superiors as you would that subordinates should be to you.

Remember that while war evokes heroism, it has also its brutalizing side, its appeal to elemental instincts. American college men today are cleaner in their lives than the youth of any other land. Do not lose your personal standards in the long, monotonous drudgery that precedes the storm of battle, in the outburst of exultation or depression that follows it, or in the pleasant relief of a short leave of absence from the front in the allurements of a great city. If you do not know the love of a pure woman now, you will after your return. It is a jewel, do not let it become to you less precious. Remember that your men too will come home, and strive to keep them from temptation. Help on every agency that seeks to give them healthy recreation in the dreary round of life in camp and trench. Encourage them to keep in touch with home, and to preserve their ideals unsullied; so that, whether you return yourself or not, your influence will have its true reward, not only in assaults repulsed and trenches won, but also in lives that may far outlast your own.

Young men who, through physical defects, are debarred from active military service often bear a heavy grief that they can take no part when their friends march away. To them I have a word to say. The nation must not only fight, but live, we trust, a long life that shall contribute to the progress of civilization and humanity. When the war is over much will have to be done in many ways, and every brain can help so long as it can work. During the Civil War there were in this neighborhood two brothers of military age, but not sound enough in health to enlist or wear a sword. Their only arm throughout their lives was voice or pen; but who shall speak lightly of the services of William and Henry James? Let the men who cannot go to the front feel as keen a call to the service of their country as those who go. They are not quit of service, but take it in another form, that of a lifelong duty that shall end only after bearing much fruit. Let them draw increased devotion from those who give the full measure of devotion; and let them prepare themselves therefor by cultivating to the utmost the talents with which they are endowed, and by strengthening character until it shall not be daunted by the weight of any task.

What is the reason of this call both to the strong and to the weak? Why is there a sound of a going in the tops of the trees? What does it mean, and why does it call to us? Except for certain German theorists and military men, no one wanted this war at the outset, and no one whatever wants it now. Yet war is here and it continues. This has been true of many wars. It was true of our Civil War, of which Lincoln truly said: "Both parties deprecated war, but one of them would make war rather than let the nation survive, and the other would accept war rather than let it perish; and the war came." War is merely a last resort when all else fails; but horrible as war is, it is better than submission, when that means a surrender of things that make civilization worth having — submission to the trampling under foot of a little neutral nation; to the drowning at sea of neutral civilians, men, women, and children; to the dropping of bombs from the sky on defenseless towns; to the systematic abduction of men, and far worse, of young women, on the ground that these things may terrify the enemy and enlarge the chance of victory, or feed the passions of a belligerent. To submit to such things, to stand by and see them done, would be an abandonment of self-respect by any great nation, a confession of unfitness to take an honorable part in the life of mankind. We must fight that such things shall never be done again.

We have been told in the past — and in the present — by a few people who cannot see the signs of the times or read the handwriting upon the wall, that this is a European war in which we have no interest, and in which we have no ground for interference. But, if the war in Europe should end in the triumph of autocracy bent upon going forth conquering and to conquer, we should of necessity be the object of a future attack. If a part of our land were not actually the scene of the devastation that has occurred in Belgium, France, and Servia, it would only be because we had transformed it into an armed camp, and stood perpetually on guard, straining for the purpose resources that ought to be used in bettering the conditions of life.

Moreover, nations with the same political and social ideals must stand together to defend their principles when attacked, or both they and their principles will be destroyed like a bundle of sticks separately broken. Does anyone think that when the Turks, at the high tide of their advance, beleaguered Vienna, and John Sobieski, King of Poland, marched to raise the siege, that it was not his quarrel, and that he had no ground for interference?

We are not fighting that any nation may recover territory or exact an indemnity. We are fighting to strike down a policy of military aggression, of an aggrandizement by conquest, of maltreatment of the weak by the strong; but after an unrighteous aggressor is beaten he must be compelled to do justice to those he has injured. If a robber seizes my purse, or that of another, and I grapple with him and overcome him, I do not permit him to retain the purse, although I am fighting him not for the money, but to apprehend him that he may not rob again. We must fight by the side of our allies until we can inaugurate a reign of justice and peace in the world; until, to use Lincoln's words, we "may achieve and cherish a just and lasting peace among ourselves and with all nations."

There is a sound of a going in the tops of the trees, and we must bestir ourselves, for we believe that the sound comes from the Lord, who, in his inscrutable providence, has given man a free will that permits evil things to be done, but leaves also in the hands of men power to right the wrongs of mankind. We wrestle not against flesh and blood, but against principalities, against powers, against spiritual wickedness in high places. We are to fight for righteousness, not from malice against the people of any land. So long as a people maintain a system that strikes at the welfare of the rest of mankind, war must be waged against them; although the bonds of nationality are such that for the time they cannot help it. It is the tragedy of national life that it may be a man's duty to his country to take up arms for a cause that is in fact baneful. Often he does not, and cannot, know that it is such. He merely follows his flag and the leaders in whom he trusts. He believes that he is battling for the right; but if the cause itself is evil he must be resisted even unto death. What an infinite pathos in the world that men should lay down their lives in a cause that they do not understand, conducted by measures of which they are misinformed, and accompanied by acts of barbarity of which they may be unaware.

Our people have had the advantages of an opportunity, at least, for comparatively calm judgment. This country stood aloof watching the conflict without violent passion, until slowly convinced of the full justice of the course on which it is now embarked. The nation, as a whole, began with no strong prepossession for the Allies — certainly with no desire to take up arms in their behalf, and did not decide to do so until aware that the war was deliberately carried on in violation of neutral rights, and of principles of international law and humanity which have been respected in the wars of civilized countries in recent times. Having come to this conclusion, we have joined the Allies in a cause common to us all.

Hitherto, this our cause has been maintained by those who are now our companions in arms. For nearly three years they have borne the brunt of the battle, have shed their blood and suffered grievously. The Belgian and Servian soldiers have been swept from their land by overwhelming odds. Millions of Russians have fallen silently in a stubborn fight. The whole British Empire has poured out its manhood on land and sea; and France has been bleeding until her noble face has grown paler and paler from loss of blood. If the principles in which we have faith, for which we think we stand as a nation, are to be maintained, and a system that we deem pernicious is to be overcome, we must throw into the conflict all the force at our command. If we do so, there can be no doubt of the result.

We have waited until we heard clearly the sound of a going in the tops of the mulberry trees and then bestirred ourselves, believing that it is a call to us; not to hatred and bitterness, not to enjoyment in the sufferings of any man, but to the defense of our heritage of civilization, and to the achievement of a world where such wars shall be no more.

June 16, 1918

Now faith is the substance of things hoped for, the evidence of things not seen.

For by it the elders obtained a good report.

Through faith we understand that the worlds were framed by the word of God, so that things which are seen were not made of things which do appear.

But without faith it is impossible to please him: for he that cometh to God must believe that he is, and that he is a rewarder of them that diligently seek him.

By faith Noah, being warned of God of things not seen as yet, moved with fear, prepared an ark to the saving of his house; by the which he condemned the world, and became heir of the righteousness which is by faith.

By faith Abraham, when he was called to go out into a place which he should after receive for an inheritance, obeyed; and he went out, not knowing whither he went.

By faith he sojourned in the land of promise, as in a strange country, dwelling in tabernacles with Isaac and Jacob, the heirs with him of the same promise:

For he looked for a city which hath foundations whose builder and maker is God.

These all died in faith, not having received the promises, but having seen them afar off, and were persuaded of them, and embraced them, and confessed that they were strangers and pilgrims on the earth.

By faith Moses, when he was come to years, refused to be called the son of Pharaoh's daughter;

Choosing rather to suffer affliction with the people of God, than to enjoy the pleasures of sin for a season;

Esteeming the reproach of Christ greater riches than the treasures in Egypt: for he had respect unto the recompence of the reward.

By faith he forsook Egypt, not fearing the wrath of the king: for he endured, as seeing him who is invisible.

Through faith he kept the passover, and the sprinkling of blood, lest he that destroyed the firstborn should touch them.

By faith they passed through the Red sea as by dry land: which the Egyptians assaying to do were drowned.

And what shall I more say? for the time would fail me to tell of Gedeon, and of Barak, and of Samson, and of Jephthae; of David also, and Samuel, and of the prophets:

Who through faith subdued kingdoms, wrought righteousness, obtained promises, stopped the mouths of lions,

Quenched the violence of fire, escaped the edge of the sword, out of weakness were made strong, waxed valiant in fight, turned to flight the armies of the aliens.

Women received their dead raised to life again: and others were tortured, not accepting deliverance; that they might obtain a better resurrection:

And others had trial of cruel mockings and scourgings, yea, moreover of bonds and imprisonment:

They were stoned, they were sawn asunder, were tempted, were slain with the sword: they wandered about in sheepskins and goatskins; being destitute, afflicted, tormented;

(Of whom the world was not worthy:) they wandered in deserts, and in mountains, and in dens and caves of the earth.

And these all, having obtained a good report through faith, received not the promise:

God having provided some better thing for us, that they without us should not be made perfect.

Wherefore seeing we also are compassed about with so great a cloud of witnesses, let us lay aside every weight, and the sin which doth so easily beset us, and let us run with patience the race that is set before us.

HEBREWS 11:1–3, 6–10, 13, 24–29, 32–40; 12:1.

JEHOVAH was the tribal God of the Jews, and even after the sublime conception developed of a universal ruler of the world, and of all mankind, the Jews remained his peculiar people. Hence the national heroes had a sacred as well as a patriotic character. Patriotism had a religious quality, and sacrifice for the nation was attributed to religious zeal. It is natural, therefore, that the examples of faith in this chapter should have a patriotic significance and that many of them should be what we should regard as instances of secular patriotism or valor. Gideon, Barak, Samson, and Jephthah were warriors, and Samson at least had very little that was saintly about him. They were captains who led their people in arms, vanquished their enemies, and saved the Israelites from oppression. Yet they are cited as examples of the power of faith.

An American filled with the same spirit as the author of the Epistle to the Hebrews might write something like this. By faith Columbus sailed across the unknown waters trusting to find land at the other side. By faith the Pilgrim Fathers migrated to the new world, seeking a home for a free exercise of their religion. By faith the frontiersmen penetrated deeper and deeper into the wilderness until the whole continent was opened to civilization. By faith Washington endured the hardships of Valley Forge that a new and independent nation might survive. By faith the framers of the Constitution devised a form of government that this nation might be united, prosperous, and permanent. By faith Lincoln persevered through the dark days of the Civil War, that the unity of the nation might be preserved and slavery abolished. By faith Fulton invented the steamboat, and Morse the telegraph. By faith Morton, yearning to reduce human suffering, relieved pain through anaesthesia, and made modern surgery possible. By faith Dr. Carroll offered himself up for exposure, and died, to take away the scourge of Yellow Fever. And what shall we say of others who by faith have planted industries, built railroads, made inventions and discoveries, added to knowledge, healed the sick, purified politics, and improved social relations, of whom often the world was not worthy.

Had these men faith? Not necessarily faith in the sense of a belief in the articles of a fixed religious creed; but faith in the sense of a conviction that an object was worth the unswerving devotion of a life. Without such a faith no great achievement is possible. With it, if unselfish, no object is devoid of deep moral significance. The essence of such a faith is a steadfast moral purpose. The object may, in the eyes of the world, be great or small, the part played by the man of faith may be large or subordinate, but if pursued from moral motives, to the utmost of his capacity and opportunity, it is for that man an act of faith and of devotion, and I believe that he will in no wise lose his reward.

Some seeds of a faith fall by the wayside and the birds devour them. These men never know that they have almost seen a vision. They are not aware of the chance of the higher manhood that has escaped them. Some seeds fall on stony ground and quickly spring up, but soon fade away. This is the case of unstable souls who have no root in themselves, no deep convictions, who put their hand to the plow and look back. Some fall among thorns, and the seed is choked by the superficial pleasures and cares of life. These men have no true perspective, no sense of proportion. In youth they enjoy life, but find later how little they have made of it, how far they are from what they might have been. They are not usually bad. They are simply indifferent, unperceptive, lacking imagination or persistence, often useful when strongly led in a good cause, but without sufficient power of self-direction.

I spoke of those who put their hand to the plow, and look back. That is a natural instinct, but in speaking of them I do not refer to those who hesitate from regret at the sacrifices their chosen path entails, who shrink from heroism because it is costly. Those are the cheaper souls. I refer to the more noble natures who are self-distrustful, who are haunted by doubts whether after all the work they have undertaken is worth while, whether it is not beyond their powers, whether the door of opportunity is really open to them, and whether they are not making a failure of their task. Everyone, not supremely self-confident, goes through this stage, often more than once. The day comes when a man must grit his teeth, persevere in spite of discouragements, and have faith though hope grows dim. It is well to think maturely before taking up any work that calls for the devotion of a life; and when entered upon a decision may have to be reviewed in the light of new facts. In that sense the mind should always be open; but it is not always easy to distinguish between a rational doubt based upon greater knowledge of the subject or a larger view of life, and a hesitation caused by hope deferred. When night comes on, one must pursue the course laid out in daylight; and the time often comes when, in spite of obstacles that seem to increase as he advances, a man must assume that his former decision was right, with faith in his own past judgment until the dawn breaks upon him again. Mere shadows across the path, thrown by discouragement, must not be confused with pitfalls. They are dark places that must be expected and must be crossed without slackening speed. It is not always possible to see the distant hills. The clouds may lower, or the fog shut out the view; but one can always see the compass and the map. It is not always possible to behold the vision clearly. It may often fade or be dimmed, but one can always hold the faith in it, and if one presses forward on the road it will reappear nearer and more distinct.

Someone may suppose that these things do not come to a soldier in war. Yet in a camp and in the field there is drudgery, disappointment, and a sense of poor success. There is, indeed, no possibility of turning back; but it is easy to lose enthusiasm and energy, to fail to keep oneself at the top notch, although this is needed for the best achievement on one's own part, and on that of the unit to which one belongs. The all-important thing is the morale of the troops, and this depends upon the living faith of the men and especially of the officers; the faith that never falters or slackens, and that is ever freshly contagious, whether work is stimulating or dull, in the exhaustion following victory or in the gloom of repulse.

I have said that the faithful shall in no wise lose his reward. This does not mean that he always wins what seems to the world success. If we read the account of the crucifixion in the Gospel of St. Mark as we should read another history, we feel that the last cry of Christ upon the cross showed that he had a deep sense of failure; and we are certainly given to understand that the disciples believed at the time that his mission had been a failure. Yet they soon saw things in their true light and perceived that his death was essential to his mission. Many of the greatest human benefactors have died supposing they had failed. If Lincoln had been murdered a month earlier he would have died without knowing that his work had been successful. If he had died in the preceding August he would have left his work unfinished, in grave doubt whether it had not wholly failed.

The chapter in the Epistle to the Hebrews, after reciting the examples of faith among the benefactors of the race, ends by telling us that all these died in faith not having received the promise. To few men is it given to fulfill wholly their vision, for the inspiration of a vision comes from its difficulty. Many men never see how much they have really achieved, and although they have done much and brought the end nearer for others to attain, they die lamenting their unsuccess. Yet a man's work is truly judged not by himself but only by omniscience. We are single links in a long chain of which we cannot see the end. On the monument to the Wesley brothers in Westminster Abbey are inscribed Wesley's own words, "God buries his workmen, but carries on his work."

Happy is the warrior who gives his life in a just cause, because those who die after a long life of struggle may be to the end harassed by doubts about the success of their efforts; but the soldier who has done his duty knows that his death, though a misfortune, can never be a failure.

June 15, 1919

... why are they then baptized for the dead?
I CORINTHIANS 15:29.

WHETHER it is proper or not in a sermon to take for the text a passage used in an entirely different sense from that which it has in the Bible, I do not know. To whatever custom of the early church St. Paul referred when he wrote of baptizing for the dead, it has no relation to the thoughts I want to present to you.

On Baccalaureate Sunday, substantially the whole class is habitually gathered here. But this year the ranks are thinned. Many who entered the army are still with the colors, many others have been discharged but have not returned to college, and nineteen former members of the class have fallen in the war. These are the men we cannot help thinking of today, and we ask ourselves what we owe to their memory and what guidance we can obtain from their devotion.

Their work in life is done, their service is complete, as ours will never be. They consecrated their life to a cause and gave it all. The service of the living can hardly be so full and perfect. The record of those who have fallen cannot be marred by weakness, by error, or mischance. It stands forever sacred, glowing with the fire of youth, a beacon for all that shall hereafter walk beneath the college elms.

Their lives were freely offered and were taken, while others who offered as freely were spared for something more. The fate of those who died was the more heroic, that of the living more continuous and more perplexing. The soldier obeys commands; the citizen must find his own path in an unknown future and with insufficient light. It is they, the soldier dead, who died in the light, and we who live on in the dusk; for to them was given to see their duty clearly and follow it to the end, while we must grope for ours in the twilight through a labyrinth.

Some people of generous enthusiasm have believed that the unselfish purpose, the lofty ideals, the inspiration, generated by this war will prove permanent, and raise men to a height of character that will transform our nation and keep it on a higher plane. But history gives little warrant for such an expectation. The wars of Napoleon were followed by a race for wealth, by an exploitation of the inventions in machinery and of the laboring classes under the new factory system. Our own Civil War, with its lofty humanitarian desire to give freedom to the slave, was succeeded by an era of political degradation that reached its lowest point in the corruption of the Tweed Ring in New York. Nor is this surprising. The waste of war — and there has never been waste comparable to that in the track of this war — leaves devastation, losses, and debts to be made good, and it is natural that men's minds should be for a time engrossed by material aims. Beside the general damage to be repaired, men feel that they must care for their own families, restore their comforts, and make provision for their future. Moreover it is a fact of human nature, taught by experience of things both great and small, that a vehement moral effort is apt to be followed by moral lassitude. Great wars, therefore, are liable to be succeeded by a period of materialism and moral relaxation. That is a danger to be guarded against today. We can see it already on the horizon. The speed with which the unselfish ardor of the war has faded, and the motives of ordinary life have supervened, has been a shock to many people. Everywhere we shall need moral convictions, strongly held and sustained by strenuous moral effort.

The world of men is ever in unstable equilibrium, rising or falling in the moral scale. It cannot stand still, but must become better or worse; and its fate depends upon the visions of young men, and the extent to which they make their visions true. The future is in their hands, and probably at an earlier date than they are themselves aware. The more so because, by virtue of their service in the war, they are likely soon to exert a greater public influence than they would otherwise possess; and because the association in a common army life has brought about among young men a solidarity of opinion, a means of influencing one another, which would not have been acquired in peaceful times.

The danger to most men, that which keeps them from living on the highest plane of which they are capable, is not usually crude temptation to gross evil, but the conventional, and therefore mediocre, standards that surround them. It is easy for a man of ordinary good intentions to resist a palpable wrong, to keep his hands from stealing and his tongue from deliberate lying. It is another thing not to be misled by the statement that "everybody does so," and that "one cannot be better than the world he lives in." These assertions are not true. Not everybody does questionable things because others do them. There are always to be found those who do not. A man can be better than the world he lives in. There are many who are; all honor be to them.

It is those who are better than the world about them that make the world a better place for themselves and for others. Mankind is raised by the comparatively small number of men who are above the conventional standard of their day. Mark you, those who are better, not those who think themselves better, or profess to be better, or desire to be esteemed better. The best men I have known have been little conscious of the fact, for they have compared themselves, not with others, but with an inner standard higher than they felt they could attain. They were thinking, not how they appeared, but what they were, and what they might be.

A man need not be a general to be a good soldier and a hero. A man need not be a public character, or a martyr, to be a good citizen and a force for righteousness. The more good men in public life the better, and where shall we find them if not among those who in youth have fought for what they held precious in civilization. Never before has the world, or our own country, had more need of statesmen to direct the current of thought and action, than in the period of readjustment that lies before us; never more use for brave men and true, concerned, not about office, political career, or party advantage, but about integrity, good service, and wise judgment in the government; never a stronger call for people who can think clearly and speak fearlessly.

Yet the influence of most men upon the world is exerted not so much in the conduct of public affairs as in their profession or occupation. Those who maintain a low standard there, cutting as close to the border line of positive misconduct as possible without crossing it, are dragging down the moral tone of that profession or business, and with it that of the whole community of which it is a part. Those who maintain the conventional standard merely, are the neutrals, the slackers, in the war between good and evil; while those who maintain a high standard, who despise what is unworthy, and strive to work on something better than the conventional plane, confer upon their profession, and through it upon the whole community, a benefit of incalculable value.

There is, I know, a widespread belief that a man who in worldly affairs tries to be better than his day, courts failure. This is no more true than the opposite maxim that in business honesty is the best policy. From the point of view of worldly success, of money making, dishonesty sometimes succeeds and sometimes does not. The bad often prosper and so do the good; and although the public is prone to whitewash success, that does not affect the moral nature of the process by which it was obtained. The wisdom of the serpent is not a guide in moral questions, nor are these to be judged by material results. If honesty is often the best policy, that is not the reason for being honest; and if shrewd overreaching prospers, that is no excuse for its adoption. Moreover, we must not judge even of the result as the world judges. What it deems a defeat is sometimes a victory. To the world of their day, Herod was a success and John the Baptist a failure, Pilate was a success and Christ a failure. The heroes of history have often been unpopular, sometimes martyrs; and yet have succeeded in accomplishing what they undertook to do. If your aim is material, the world will estimate your success correctly, but in so far as your aim is higher, you must look elsewhere for judgment.

While speaking of success and failure, let me add a caution for those who are liable to discouragement by early rebuffs of fortune. A young man does not always start out upon the path where his capacities and opportunities give him the greatest advantages, or he meets with unexpected obstacles that bar his path. Sometimes he feels himself beaten and becomes disheartened. Let him remember that in the ventures of life a failure is usually not important if one does not accept it as final. To expect to go through life without failure is like expecting to play a game and make every move perfectly; like expecting to solve problems and never make a mistake. Prepare as thoroughly as possible to avoid failure, but when it comes do not surrender to fate in despair. The effect of a failure depends upon what we do about it. Almost everyone fails and fails constantly, and sometimes those who have failed most are in the end the most successful.

I said that men who live upon a high moral plane confer upon the whole community a benefit of incalculable value, and this is true. It is they who raise the moral tone, who, indeed, keep it from being dragged down by the sordid aims which never lack people to promote them. It was not fanciful, but, like many things in the Bible, a universal truth embodied in a narrative, that Sodom would have been saved if it had contained ten good men, uncorrupted by the low conventional standards of the town.

Our young men have shown in this war how large is the number of those who, under the impulse of a great cause, are heroic. If they could keep themselves on that plane throughout life, they would be a race of giants; and anyone who does so, raises the level of many more about him. He sets a standard for those with whom he comes in contact, and helps those who desire to live up to their ideals but in the rough path of life find it hard to do it. The men who have seen the vision, who have been eager to risk their lives in a great crusade, must never let the inspiration fade into the light of common day. They must have within themselves a holy of holies where the fire is ever burning and the compass of life is kept secure. There is no better way of retaining the vision undimmed than by keeping fresh in memory those who gave their lives for it, who died with faith in their mission in their hearts, and with its light shining in their eyes.

This is what I mean by being baptized for the dead. It is consecrating ourselves to the resistance of evil which they died in overthrowing, to the making of a better world on a higher moral plane which their last service has made possible. As they died for us, let us resolve to live for them and for the hope in which they died.

June 20, 1920

Now the word of the Lord came unto Jonah the son of Amittai, saying,
Arise, go to Nineveh, that great city, and cry against it; for their wickedness is come up before me.
JONAH 1:1, 2.

NARRATIVES are of two kinds. One of them, history, deals with real events; the other, fiction, with imaginary ones. This last, when used to inculcate a moral, we call fable or parable. The Bible is full of both kinds of narratives. In the New Testament they are in general easily distinguished. No one supposes that the parable of the Lost Sheep, of the Talents, or of the Prodigal Son describes an actual occurrence. In the Old Testament, on the other hand, the book itself does not always tell us whether it deals with history or fiction, and the class to which it belongs must be gathered from its contents. Hence it is that writings, really parables, have sometimes been taken for history, and thereby provoked needless criticism and difficulty. The book of Jonah is a case in point. Much popular discussion has been expended on the question whether a fish — by tradition turned into a whale — could really swallow a man whole or not; whereas a candid study of the book seems to make it clear that the story is a parable. The very episode of the fish points to this, for such a tale of a man living in a sea monster and afterwards relating his experience is not unknown in ancient fiction. But quite apart from that, the course of the other events — the sudden conversion of the Ninevites, the gourd which grew up in a night and perished in a day, the very rapidity of the action, developing just as is required for the dramatic sequence and the moral lesson — appears to show the same nature of the composition.

If the book is a parable intended to inculcate a moral, we can well inquire what lesson it is designed to teach, for the moral may be no less important today than in the remote period when the book was written. Jonah was a reformer who felt that he had a mission to rebuke the immorality, the material motives, the levity, and the lack of serious purpose in the great city of his time. But he shrank from doing so. He found it hard to nerve himself for the uncongenial task. He sought to occupy himself with other things, or, as the writer describes it, he tried to flee from the presence of God. But in vain. Even on the sea he could not escape; and at last his conscience, as we should say today, forced him to do his duty. At the second call he went to Nineveh. What was his mission there? Obviously to call the people to repentance. Never, as you may observe, was he informed that Nineveh would be destroyed, or even directed to threaten the people with overthrow. But it was, of course, understood that calamity would befall them if they did not repent — yet clearly only if they did not do so. The object was repentance, not destruction. The threat of the consequences of their sin was the means of bringing about reform. It was the argument Jonah was to use, the weapon he was to employ; but he had the threat so firmly fixed in his mind that it became the subject of his prophecy and he lost from sight the ultimate object for which it was to be used.

He went to Nineveh and foretold the destruction of the city. His preaching was so powerful that to his astonishment the whole people immediately repented in sackcloth and ashes. The object of his mission was accomplished with miraculous speed, the destruction of the city, which was to follow a persistence in sin, became needless and did not take place; but having foretold evil, he was disappointed that it did not come. He was angry with himself and with God, and retired to brood in solitude over the failure of his prophecy. Then follows the story of the gourd and God's explanation of the reason for sparing the city after the people had repented. The moral then is that of the man who becomes so intent upon the means of achieving his object that he mistakes the means for the end, and by his passion for it blinds himself to the good he might have accomplished, or perchance has actually attained.

Although the setting and the incidents of this parable bear little relation to the present day, the moral is singularly pertinent to the life of a forcible man in the ordinary currents of our time.

Mr. Lawrence Pearsall Jacks, in one of his writings during the war, referred to the comfort of having a plain duty to perform, with few moral questions to decide. The great object, never lost from sight during the struggle, was winning the victory; and, except for those in high authority, a man's duty was to obey orders, to carry out to the best of his ability a work laid out for him; and this was true whether he served in the armed forces or as a civilian. He had no need to trouble himself about the end to be sought; he could fix his thoughts wholly upon the means of securing it. But with the ceasing of hostilities this has changed, and therein lies one of the sources of the uncertainty, the unrest, the confusion, and the disintegration that have followed the armistice in all the countries engaged in the war, and in almost every field of political and industrial life. Unity of effort has been succeeded by dispersion of aims. Men have no longer a common object, and the peoples are groping in the twilight.

No doubt this state of things is due to the profound dislocation of normal conditions caused by the gigantic conflict, and will in time pass away; but the difference in the position of a man in war and in peace endures. In the former his course is mainly prescribed. In peace he must lay it out for himself. He is a self-directed unit. He must determine both the end he will pursue and the means of attaining it, and herein the story of Jonah is significant. Most men are tempted to make his mistake, and many fall into it — almost always unwittingly, of course, like Jonah himself. He was fully conscious that he was evading his duty when he refused to go to Nineveh, but quite unaware that he was in the wrong about anything after he went there. He believed he was at great personal sacrifice doing his duty and could not understand why God did not support him. This is constantly happening to all of us, and is the cause of many of our mistakes and discomfitures.

A man with a family of children intends, very properly, to provide for them. Perhaps in early life he had a hard struggle with poverty, and wishes to give them advantages he did not himself possess. At any rate he wants to leave them comfortable and happy. His business is exacting. It consumes his time and at the end of the day he is care-worn and tired. His affairs are prosperous, but he has not much leisure to devote to his boys. He comes to think mainly of the material possessions his children will enjoy, rather than of their character and usefulness. He is not without a strong moral sense of a negative kind. On the contrary, he is upright and scrupulous, and wishes them to be so; but he has not the time for the personal intimacy which would teach them a high standard of positive duty. In the fullness of time he dies, leaving a large fortune, and his sons lead innocent, harmless but useless lives. His aim was their welfare, and yet, by mistaking the means for the end, he has failed to make them as happy as he might. Their lives are vacant instead of being full, weak where they might be strong, poor in everything but material wealth. This is no imaginary case. One sees it every day among the sons of good men; and it often comes from fathers' being so absorbed in the means as to lose sight of the end for which alone the means was worth pursuing.

Let us take another example. A man goes into public life. He intends to serve his country to the best of his ability. Personal ambition he is ready to put aside for the nation's good. He is convinced that this good is best promoted by a certain cause or a particular party, and as time goes on this becomes so fixed in his mind that he is ready to sacrifice almost anything for its benefit. He would not for a moment stoop to dishonest or corrupt methods, but he loses his sense of proportion, and becomes a blind partisan. This again is not uncommon among good men, nor is it unknown among true reformers of an ardent type. It is perhaps the chief source of the evils in public life. Many a statesman could lament with Wolsey that he had not served his God with half the zeal he served his King.

Take again the man of science who longs to make a discovery that will advance the welfare, increase the knowledge, or enlarge the ideal of mankind. Certainly this is a noble ambition. But he finds that others are encroaching on his field, or getting the credit for his work; and at last his interest is more engaged with the fame he hopes to attain than with the benefit his discoveries will confer. This is a canker that eats away the spirit of co-operation on which scientific progress at the present day depends.

Temptations of this kind — or shall we say failures to see aright — beset everyone in every occupation, and they are most insidious because unconscious. Jonah's was the case of a man who in success lost sight of the real object of his work. The same may be true in failure. In the closing days of the Civil War, in the early morning at Appomattox, when the retreat of the army of Northern Virginia had been cut off by the Union forces, General Alexander, the chief of artillery, found General Lee sitting by a camp fire, and suggested that if he would give an order to disband and rally in the mountains of North Carolina a guerrilla warfare might be kept up indefinitely. General Lee replied that while this was true, the cause for which they had fought was lost, that the plan proposed would result in anarchy and barbarism, and they must remember that they were a civilized and Christian people. He rode away to arrange the terms of the surrender, and as these were being drawn up General Grant remarked that the Southern soldiers had better keep their horses because they would need them for the spring plowing.* Neither commander forget that the war was a means, not an end, and that the end had already been reached by victory on one side and defeat on the other.

Observe that the cases I have mentioned of losing the true end from sight are those of men essentially good. There are bad men who intend to do wrong. Of such I am not speaking. Perhaps there would be little use in preaching to them; and it is probable that the aggregate evil in the world, or rather the aggregate inability of mankind to reach a higher level, is due less to deliberate wrongdoing than to the defects of men who mean on the whole to do right. Such men fail to attain the best that is in them because they do not continually ask themselves in what that best consists. They pursue lesser aims, not because they prefer them, but because in the press and strain of events, in the cares of life, they become absorbed in immediate objects and forget the higher ones. Jonah did no harm in the parable because God disposed otherwise; but if he could have had his way he would have destroyed all the people of Nineveh, and thought he was doing right. Yet had he stopped to ask himself seriously what was the object of his mission, his own answer would certainly have been that it was to bring the Ninevites to repentance. His neglect to ask himself that question was the cause of his error. He lost sight of his object,

* This story was repeated in the Baccalaureate Sermon of June 15, 1930.

not because he could not see it, but because he did not try to.

The man who knows what he wants and how he intends to get it is very apt to succeed; and this is not more true of material aims than of higher ones. The object of true religion in every age and every clime has been to search out the ultimate end of life and reveal those things that are of eternal value, in contrast with those which are ephemeral and insignificant. Ascetics and mystics have sometimes carried their exaltation so far as to despise the things by which mankind must live, and without which it cannot rise in civilization. But the great mass of men have erred in the other direction, by seeking only the things of the present, by thinking too much of food and raiment and too little of the Kingdom of God. True religion and spiritual wisdom consist in regarding the lower as steps to the higher, without losing sight of the end to which they are only a means.

Whatever a man's opinions on religious questions may be, if he consider seriously the highest end he can have in life, and if he keep that end steadily before his mind, he will be a man of elevated character. He will be led on to ever better and more lofty aims, and help others to live upon a higher plane. If the world means more than a senseless struggle for material pleasure at the expense of others, the higher life is the only one that is worth living, and it can be attained only by keeping the ultimate goal always before the eyes.

June 19, 1921

Woe unto them that call evil good, and good evil; that put darkness for light, and light for darkness; that put bitter for sweet, and sweet for bitter!

Woe unto them that are wise in their own eyes, and prudent in their own sight!

ISAIAH 5:20, 21.

The multitude of the wise is the welfare of the world.
WISDOM 6:24.

THE FIRST of these texts is a denunciation; the second is a promise. The statements, however, are only two different aspects of a single truth. No one thinks that he is himself putting darkness for light, evil for good, or bitter for sweet; but everyone is sure that some other people are doing so; and, at the present time, that many people are doing it in a very exaggerated and dangerous way. Great numbers of good men and women are seriously alarmed today at ideas that are being propagated, and they think that by shutting their own ears and the mouths of others the danger can be escaped. They remind one of the people in Kingsley's *Water Babies*, who walked backwards crying "Don't tell us!" But surely the way to overcome a wrong opinion is not to silence it, but to show its falsity.

The world is in confusion — a natural result of the turmoil of thought and the rush of feeling that accompany and follow a great war. Men's minds are like the sea after a storm, where, although the wind has gone down, the billows still roll and break, irresistible in their huge mass, and threatening to founder even a ship that has ridden out the gale. Conditions have not yet returned to the normal; nor has the world adjusted itself to them. In such a state of bewilderment, of misunderstandings, of cross purposes, what is needed? The answer is clear thinking.

Of course everyone believes that he thinks clearly himself. So did the little Scotch girl, who said, "Grandmother, all the world is daft but thee and me, and I think thee a little queer sometimes." No one really thinks clearly unless he has thought long and profoundly; unless he comprehends the point of view of those who do not agree with him; unless he has found out the limitations of his own principles; for all theories, principles, maxims, and rules of human conduct can be carried *ad absurdum*. They all have their proper limits, because at some point they come into conflict with other principles not less true and not less limited. A doctor, for example, is sent for by a patient whose life may depend on how soon medical attendance arrives. The doctor's obvious duty is to go as quickly as possible. He goes in his auto at the utmost speed, and in so doing runs over and kills a child. Clearly we must revise the statement of the doctor's duty. He must go to the patient as quickly as is consistent, with due care not to run over someone else.

Within a few days I have been reading Professor Hart's selection of Lincoln's speeches and letters. In running through them one is impressed by the careful limitation Lincoln constantly placed upon the principles that he believed most intensely. He thought slavery morally wrong, but, while unflinchingly opposed to its extension to the Territories, he would not countenance attacks upon it in the States because he was of opinion that there it was protected by the Constitution. The principle that slavery, being wrong, should be opposed was limited by another principle that the Constitution and laws should be upheld; and he never advocated abolition by force until he felt justified in doing so on the ground that it was a proper military measure in carrying out his constitutional duty to preserve the Union. In reading his writings one sees that this was the result not of political astuteness, but of integrity of mind and clearness of thought. One principle did not blind him to another, for he perceived both, and therefore the limitations each imposed upon the other.

Let us take the principle of patriotism, the desire to promote by all possible means the prosperity of the country, the nation, the people to which one belongs. Few men are ready to deny the validity, the importance, the inviolable moral obligation of that principle. Even in the associations which, before the war, proclaimed the superior obligation of class solidarity, or so-called internationalism, there were few men who failed, when the war came, to take the part of the nation to which they belonged. There had been an expectation that the Socialists in Germany would refuse to support their government and thus prevent war; but when the war came, that did not happen. In some cases, as in Alsace-Lorraine for example, the people, or many of them, did not consider that they belonged to the country that held sway over them; but that is another question, the question to what nation patriotism is due.

Are there any limitations to the principle of patriotism? Is dishonesty, for example, is the breaking of solemn treaties, is ruthless inhumanity to a weaker neighbor, justified by a belief that it will conduce to the prosperity of one's own people? Is a nation morally right in seizing anything it can obtain by force or fraud, or has it a duty to deal fairly with others, and respect their rights? Would Cain have acted properly if, instead of being a single individual, he had been fifty millions to Abel's twenty-five millions and had called himself a nation? Is a nation under any moral obligation to abstain from acts against other nations which, if committed by a private individual, would make him an object of general abhorrence, and perhaps bring him to the gallows? Is abstaining from such acts the limit of its moral obligation, or has it any positive duties to others? In short, does the Golden Rule have any application among nations?

Treitschke proclaimed the doctrine that there is no moral obligation superior to the national interest, and many Germans adopted his ideas in whole or in part. I think it may be argued that if this conception of the State, or something akin to it, had not been prevalent in Germany it would not have been possible for any men, however close to the source of authority, to have led Germany into the war. It may at least be urged that it was this attitude of mind which furnished the backing for the attempt to take advantage by war of the situation in Europe, for invading Belgium in violation of a treaty, and for the wanton destruction of the means of recuperation in France. If it be true that the Great War was a natural result of the principle that there is no moral obligation superior to the national interest, then the blame for the ghastly suffering endured, and for all that has been suffered since and will be for years to come, lies not only with those who taught that doctrine and those who acted upon it, but also with those multitudes of great and small who accepted it and by so doing swelled the tide of popular opinion that made the war possible. Observe, I am not expressing an opinion on any of these questions. In this place it would hardly be proper for me to do so. I am merely seeking to insist upon the responsibility of every man for his opinions, by pointing out how his personal opinions go into the great scales in which the destinies of mankind are balanced.

If it be true that the war came because the people of Germany in their opinions put evil for good, darkness for light, and bitter for sweet, then we can only say of the calamities that have come upon their country as Lincoln said of the woes brought by the Civil War on both North and South, "The judgments of the Lord are true and righteous altogether." But we can add with him, "Let us judge not that we be not judged," or rather let us beware that by harboring in our own minds unsound opinions we fall not into like condemnation.

In this matter of patriotism it is the solemn duty of every man to think clearly what, if any, are its moral limitations, and what duties and responsibilities it involves. It is his duty to try to discover how far his country is limited in its moral freedom of action by the duties that it owes to other portions of mankind. Future wars, future calamities, future miseries incalculable, or, on the other hand, future prosperity, future intellectual and spiritual advance, may depend upon solving these questions aright; and by the solution of these questions I mean their solution by the balance of the opinions of all citizens as individuals.

The same thing applies in other relations of life of a public or semi-public nature. We hear much of the rights of property and of labor. Is the owner of property justified in managing it to augment his own profits, regardless of the general welfare; and is the workman justified in curtailing production if it be to the detriment of the community at large; and if not, what are the proper limitations? Again, it is not my object here to express or imply answers to such questions, but to point out that they require answers; because the tranquillity and welfare of our country depends upon their being answered aright, and no man, whatever his position in life, can wholly free himself from the responsibility for the opinions he holds about them. As a people we are highly sensitive to public opinion, and that is made up of the personal opinions held by each and all of us. We cannot, like the subjects of a despot, say that it is for the ruler, and not for us, to inquire and decide.

Most people, and perhaps in a peculiar degree the American people, tend in the busy life of the world to save themselves from strenuous thought by taking refuge in the opinions of their associates, of the men in like occupations, of the party or group to which they belong. This saves some of them, indeed, from eccentricity, and from irrational extremes, but it does not absolve men from responsibility for the correctness of their opinions, or save the nation from the consequences of their errors. The fact that others make the same mistake is no excuse. Yet people who go with the prevailing current of opinion seldom feel any personal responsibility, still less contrition, when that current leads to wrongdoing or disaster. Corporate or co-operative selfishness is today a greater danger than personal selfishness, because it is more insidious, and wears the garb of something more noble than a mere personal aim. Although men are by nature gregarious creatures, they should not — like sheep — move under the simple impulse of the mass. Man has the ability to think for himself, to weigh reasons, to forecast in some degree the future, and to reflect upon the consequences of his acts. In times like these it is of vital import that his responsibility for his individual opinions should be relentlessly asserted.

Clamor of a crowd is often mistaken for opinion. The art of producing the semblance of a public opinion by a general shout has progressed greatly within a generation. It is easy to provoke such a shout for a catchword which embodies a principle good in itself, without a perception on the part of the crowd that it has its limit and that they are in effect being urged beyond that limit. Group psychology has been studied until we are familiar with its principles and its use. Professor Dicey remarked, in criticizing the historical method of studying human problems, that when the origin of an abuse has been explained the abuse itself is half condoned. Let us not suppose that, because psychology of crowds is a fact, its results are therefore right; or that, because organization and machinery furnish a powerful weapon for propagating ideas on the part of those who believe in them, the ideas themselves are therefore correct. The weapon may be used for an unjust or unwise movement as well as for one that is just and wise.

As I have said in this place before, we are told in the Bible that the Holy Spirit will convince the world of sin, of righteousness, and of judgment, by which is meant one's own sin, and the righteousness and judgment of God; but we are too prone to think of someone else's sin, of one's own righteousness, and of judgment by popular vote.

What we need now is not more organization or more machinery, but more thought; personal thought, clear, far reaching and profound, as unbiased and illumined, and, not least, as widespread among our people as possible, for in the multitude of the wise is the welfare of the world; and where shall we look for this multitude if not among those upon whom have been lavished the best educational opportunities that our country can produce — the graduates of our colleges?

June 18, 1922

. . . they measuring themselves by themselves, and comparing themselves among themselves, are not wise.
                              II CORINTHIANS 10:12.

WHY ARE they not wise? Before we can answer that we must know what we mean by wise. Do we mean worldly wisdom, a shrewd perception of the course which will lead to material success? In that sense of the word, such a measurement by themselves, that is by one another — a guiding of conduct by the customary standards, by what the market place will tolerate, may be wise. Average honesty may be a good standard for mere money-making. The old proverb says that honesty is the best policy — meaning that it is best for purely business reasons. It may be or it may not. It may be so as a rule, but not always. A man who is honest solely because it is the best business policy is honest only from a broad perception of his own material interest, not from any moral principle. If placed in a position where a dishonest act would yield a profit and could never be discovered, or do him any worldly harm, he would have no reason, drawn from the best policy principle, to shun the dishonest act. That is if he had no sense of an inherent moral motive for being honest.

But the word wise has another meaning — a spiritual as distinguished from a worldly significance. Almost all men, and all men of character, believe that there is an intrinsic reason for moral conduct, apart from its material value to the man himself; that self-sacrifice for a worthy object is neither an irrational folly, nor a mere survival of a primitive herd instinct, but the noblest act of the most highly developed creature on the earth. The memory of the young men who died in the war is too fresh in our minds to let us think for a moment that their heroic deaths were due to a cold conviction of personal advantage or enlightened self-interest. They did not want to die; but they went forth knowing the danger, even courting it, from a profound sense of duty. No one shall persuade us that they did so from a traditional but irrational altruism, and that self-devotion is less worthy of admiration than we feel it to be. If anyone could so persuade us he would rob life of that which makes it best worth living. No one shall prevent us from glorying in those young men, or drawing from their example a firmer conviction that all life has to offer is small compared with doing what is right.

Assuming, then, that there is an imperative moral duty to do right, and that to be wise means to act in accord with that obligation, why is it that those who measure themselves by themselves, and compare themselves among themselves are not wise? Perhaps it is better to ask first why men are so prone to measure their conduct in this way. It is, in fact, a very easy standard of life. To do as others do is simple. It saves the trouble of thinking and deciding. It is a good excuse also for some relaxation of a rigorous principle, particularly when one is in a tight place. But how far is it wise from the point of view of its effect upon the public interest? Most of us have seen its results at one time or another, in business, in public affairs, in everyday life, in war, and even in sport. There is, in fact, nothing more demoralizing than the habit of palliating things which everyone knows ought not to be done, on the ground that everyone does them. A man under such conditions is apt to compare himself, not with the best, or even with the average, but with those who do the things he is only too ready to excuse in himself. In fact he is prone to believe that the rivals by whom he is measuring himself are a little worse than they really are. The tendency in any community where such a habit prevails generally is downward. The only way to lift the world is for men of character to act up to their principles, although it be to their own loss; and by their example provoke others to do likewise. A good example is as contagious as a bad one.

How about its consequences for the man himself? We know very well that some people who act on their principles without regard to the opinions of others do not do either the community or themselves much good. We call them fanatics or cranks, and are more inclined to censure than admire them. Such men are not necessarily superior in moral standards to others; but are simply lacking in good judgment. The difficulty with them is not that their zeal is excessive, but that their aim is defective. Their very eccentricity attracts attention, making people feel, and what is worse, making the fanatics themselves feel, that they live up to their principles more than other men who are really quite as conscientious but more sensible. In forming one's own principles of conduct it is proper to consider, not what most men do, but what most men sincerely believe that men ought to do. This is wise, not in order to conform to other men's standards of conduct, but to obtain light in forming one's own standard; to avoid narrow, partial, and prejudiced opinions; to insure so far as possible that one sees clearly and fully all the considerations on which his opinions ought to be based. But when he has reached his opinion of what is right and wrong; when he has framed his standard of moral conduct; a man must act upon it without flinching. Let every man be firmly persuaded in his own mind, and happy is he that condemneth not himself in that thing which he alloweth; for if he swerve from what he believes to be right because others do the same he lowers his own moral tone and weakens his own moral fiber. If self-sacrifice be admirable and not foolish, if there be such a thing as moral obligation, it is because there is a moral order in the universe; and if there be such a moral order it must be for every man's ultimate welfare to conform thereto. Whether he call his belief in a moral order, and the duties it involves, a philosophy, a theology, or a faith, he throws away all that is best worth having if he fails to act upon it; and if he permits himself to be beguiled into a departure from it by thinking that he cannot be much to blame for doing what many others do, he certainly is not wise.

Everyone is familiar with the parable of the talents, and how the man with one talent who failed to use it was condemned and cast into outer darkness. Sometimes one can wish that the story had been differently told, that it had been the man with five talents who had neglected to use them to the fullest extent, and had therefore been condemned, for to whom much has been committed of him will be required the more. Duties lie upon a man according to his power for good and evil. Those who can do only little must do that little, and great is their merit if they do it faithfully. Those whose influence is wider must use it to the full for good, and great is their desert if they do so, but great also is their deficiency if they neglect their opportunities. Even in a democracy, and in any form of civil polity that has ever existed or can be conceived, power is not evenly distributed. Public office gives power, business positions and wealth do the same, and so do knowledge and the possession of a trained mind. Strangely enough the word talents which is used in the parable to denote a sum of money has now come to signify mental capacity. So much the better for our purpose, because it gives point to the appropriate moral here. Many of the men before me will have important business positions, many will have wealth in greater or less degree, not a few, the more the better, will hold public office, and many more will, I hope, take an active part in public affairs; but all possess knowledge and trained minds beyond the average, and therefore of such college men much is required.

Not always immediately, but ultimately, mankind is led by those whose thinking is clear, conscientious and generous; and never in its history has the world been more in need of such thinking than it is now. By now I do not mean only during the next half a dozen years, but during the period when the men who are now graduating will be in a position to exert their influence in the fullest measure. Civilization cannot be independent of the material instruments of which it makes use, and the increase in man's control of, and ability to apply, the forces of nature has been greater during the last hundred years than in any preceding twenty centuries of the world's history. A little over a hundred years ago horses supplied, as in the days of the Romans, the most rapid means of conveying men, merchandise, or intelligence. Wind was the only power for crossing the sea. Today anything of public interest that happens in any civilized country is known in every newspaper office over the earth almost as soon as it occurs. A man's voice can now be heard all over this country, and soon will be audible over the whole world. Flight across the Atlantic is an accomplished fact; and during the Great War we sent a million armed men to Europe in a few months. Civilization has always been deeply influenced by inventions. No one can doubt what a change was wrought in the ancient world by the use of metals. The improvement of transportation by land and water enlarged trade, and trade brought intercourse, with its new relations, its enlarged horizon, and its temptations to foreign conquest, until the sailing ship and the mariner's compass opened the whole world to the people of Europe. It has been pointed out that the invention of firearms and especially of cannon destroyed the feudal organization of society, because the baron's castle was no longer a refuge difficult to capture. The extent to which the recent progress in applied science will affect both the relation of men to one another and the interdependence of different peoples is as yet unknown; nor will it be wholly settled for a generation to come, even if no further scientific discoveries and inventions are made. Who will determine these new relations aright? Upon whom will the guidance for better or worse rest? Obviously upon the intelligent, the educated, and the public spirited people of the world. Will they set themselves earnestly to this gigantic task, or will they immerse themselves in their private pursuits and pleasures and let things drift?

By the benefactions of people dead and living, filled with far-sighted generosity, you have been trained, not only for your own benefit, but also for service to the country where you have been born. There lies the most vital point. John Harvard, and the benefactors who followed him, whose example has been followed in a host of other colleges, were inspired by a desire to help their own community, but they had no conception of the vast area over which the seed they nourished would bear fruit. When the earlier colleges were planted, the small settlements on the Atlantic seaboard were laboriously pushing their way from the shore into the forest; but now their graduates go forth across the long range of hills into the vast plains beyond and through the Rocky Mountains to the western ocean. They can, if they will, influence the destiny of the Continent. Then the few people were of one stock. Now all the races of Europe have crowded into the land. We hear much talk of the American spirit, as if it were a thing fixed and done, but it is still in the making and will be for many years to come. Shall it be a chaos of jarring self-interests, to which each race and each class contributes its harsher notes, or shall it be a harmony of what is best in each? The question will not soon have its final answer, and that answer will depend less upon the generation which is passing away than on that which is now coming on the stage. Even men now young may not see all that will come in the fullness of time. Our forefathers planted the seed, our fathers cultivated it, and we must carry on the work even though

> It may not be our lot to wield
> The sickle in the ripened field;
> Nor ours to hear on summer eves
> The reaper's song among the sheaves.

The problems before us are not those of our own land alone, but of the world. The Great War has partly caused and partly revealed a vast change in the position of our country. It has been like a young giant, boasting of his strength, yet in fact only half aware of his real force. The war and the events that followed have shown that the United States, with her resources in men and nature, has become a power unmatched in the world. Other nations are looking to it as they have hardly looked to another people before. It is no small thing to have power to influence the fate of all mankind. With power comes opportunity and with opportunity responsibility. Our own right hand may yet teach us terrible things. Our power is likely to grow still greater in the world, and what do we want our nation to become? Shall we be satisfied with material wealth and comfort, or do we desire a higher destiny? In the ancient world there were two peoples, both commercial, both prosperous, both powerful in their day, and both at last conquered by the

Romans. One of them, the Greeks, led the way for all later European peoples in art, in literature, in philosophy, and in science. The other, the Carthaginians, have left nothing, and all we know of them comes from the histories of their conquerors. A nation is what its people make it.

If we could retain the fervor and devotion that our young men displayed in the war, and which they would put forth again in a national crisis; if we could retain that spirit in the slow, hard labors of peace; if their exaltation should never fade in the light of common day, we could be the greatest people that ever dwelt upon the earth. This is not to be achieved by men's comparing themselves among themselves, or measuring themselves by an average standard; but by living up to the best they know and measuring themselves by their own highest aspiration. Nor should such men be discouraged because they are not always understood. In the words of Oliver Wendell Holmes —

> Thus drifting afar to the dim vaulted caves
> Where life and its ventures are laid,
> The dreamers who gaze while we battle the waves
> May see us in sunshine or shade;
> Yet true to our course, though our shadow grow dark,
> We'll trim our broad sail as before,
> And stand by the rudder that governs the bark,
> Nor ask how we look from the shore!

June 17, 1923

For other foundation can no man lay than that is laid, which is Jesus Christ.

Now if any man build upon this foundation gold, silver, precious stones, wood, hay, stubble;

Every man's work shall be made manifest: for the day shall declare it, because it shall be revealed by fire; and the fire shall try every man's work of what sort it is.

If any man's work abide which he hath built thereupon, he shall receive a reward.

If any man's work shall be burned, he shall suffer loss: but he himself shall be saved; yet so as by fire.

I CORINTHIANS 3:11–15.

MEN of religious and moral earnestness have sought to attain the perfect life by two different paths — contemplation and service.

Let us not hastily reject either. Christ sent forth his disciples two and two for service, but he also said that Mary who, while her sister served, sat at his feet and heard his words had chosen the good part.

All the great religions of the world have commended both attitudes, while placing more emphasis on one than the other, or an emphasis on each varying at different times. It was in a period of Christianity when a life of contemplation was more revered than philanthropic service that was coined the phrase *Laborare est orare*.

Nor is it needful to separate the two. The most active men are not always the least thoughtful, or the most meditative backward in good works. Solitude is not essential to contemplation; the Greek philosophers were constantly engaged in teaching and disputation. For most men profound thought is stimulated both by contemplation and interchange of ideas, each in seasonable measure.

Today we live in an age of action, rather than of contemplation, perhaps excessively so, and therefore St. Paul's words appeal to us. They have in fact a peculiarly modern ring, for the first impression they produce is that of measuring the value of acts by the results attained rather than by the moral purpose involved. We are prone to rate among the virtuous those who have conferred benefits upon mankind regardless of the motives that actuated them; and the effect is good, in so far as it encourages others to do the like. But this is not the attitude expressed by St. Paul in the text. He is treating only of works done for what he esteems the highest possible motive, for he speaks of building upon "this foundation" of morality, saying that no other can any man lay. He assumed the moral purpose.

Observe also, for the same reason, that he is not contrasting good acts with evil ones. It is not the comparison of the sheep and the goats; of the good man whose works will follow him, and the bad man who will be weighed down by them. He is discriminating among different works all well intentioned; among those which he compares to gold, silver, precious stones, wood, hay, and stubble, although all done from moral motives; in other words between good works of high, of moderate, or of trifling value, and he rates them according to their enduring quality when tried by fire. It is this that gives the serious aspect to his statement of the severe ordeal to which a good man's good works will be subjected.

Every man's work is in fact tried by fire, that is, by the most searching test which, in the lapse of time, can be applied. What is trivial or ephemeral is soon destroyed, while that which has permanent merit will endure. It is a laudable ambition to strive to achieve results of lasting value, although these are by no means always the ones that bulk largest at the time or are the most conspicuous. If fame delight you, if to be talked about, to have your name and portrait in the public press, the object is not difficult to attain for people who care about it, and will devote some effort and a little skill thereto. Verily they have their reward, and one that, like riches and other worldly prizes, is a gratification to those whose hearts are set upon it; but in the sight of God not to be compared with work, inconspicuous perhaps to men, that has been built into the permanent fabric of other human souls. If your aim be more than selfish gratification, if it be to accomplish something that will make men happier and better, then the more enduring its effects the more it is worth doing. It may be done in any line of human activity. It may be done, indeed is most commonly done, in connection with earning a livelihood. One does not have to seek strange paths to find it, for it lies close at hand in every familiar field of endeavor; not only in the great arts, sciences, and literature, but in the professions and in business of all kinds. The man who carries on his work, whatever it may be, with a clear view of its total effect for good upon the community; the upright man who so conducts himself that if others followed his example the world would live upon a higher plane; the man who so brings up his children, or others committed to his charge, that they can never lose the lofty principles he has given them; instills an influence that will spread from generation to generation far beyond his sight. Much of the good in our natures has come to us mediately from men and women we never saw, of whom sometimes we have never heard; and anyone may do the same for others yet unborn.

What if a man strive for the good that is enduring but does not succeed? What if his efforts are frustrated by his own mistakes or by circumstances beyond his control? St. Paul does not speak of this. He says that if any man's work shall be burned, he shall suffer loss: but he himself shall be saved; yet so as by fire. The man of whom he says this is one who has done a perishable work. How about him who seeks to build solidly but fails? The work that he has not done is left undone, but if this be from lack of tools or opportunity, and not from negligence or moral fault, he can expect to hear the judgment, "well done, good and faithful servant," for that comes as the reward not of success, but of moral effort.

Moreover, let us not forget certain facts about success which are not always borne in mind when passing hasty judgments on our fellows. It has been asserted by military critics that a nation is never finally beaten in war until it believes itself beaten. With not less accuracy it may be said that so long as a man lives he has not failed unless he believes that he has failed. Mark! believes that he has failed, or perhaps one ought to say believes that he is a failure, not is convinced that some particular effort, adventure, or plan of his has failed. The difference is vital. The man who runs his head repeatedly into the same stone wall has the kind of head least likely to be affected by the process. He shows perseverance, but not determination to succeed. Wisdom consists in changing the method as the result of experience while retaining the object; or to state the same thing in a larger way, if the purpose of a man in life is to do something of real value, and after sufficient trial he becomes convinced that his abilities or circumstances do not justify a belief that he can do so in the direction that he first proposed, he is not a failure if he strike out undiscouraged on another line.

This has been the case in some of the most fruitful careers. Many successful men have failed in the pursuit in which they finally became eminent, or in some other, before they learned how and where to apply their strength. Every schoolboy is familiar with the story of Robert Bruce, taking courage when he saw the spider spin her web on the seventh trial. Abraham Lincoln's early life was far from promising. Twice he attempted to conduct a local store only to have the enterprise come to a hopeless end in a few months. Goodyear tried one experiment after another before he hit upon the method of treating rubber that has made it one of the essential substances in the civilization of the present day. Captain Mahan applied to one publisher after another to print his book on the "Influence of Sea Power on History"; but all in vain, so that he was on the point of giving up the attempt, when Parkman, it is said, persuaded Little, Brown & Company to take it. Even then it had a scant sale, until its merit was recognized in England, and in a few years he became the contemporary American writer best known abroad. To come nearer home, our late benefactor, Henry L. Higginson, in early life studied music for several years in Europe, but finding himself unfitted for a musical career, came home shortly before the Civil War. Severely wounded as a cavalry officer in the Army of the Potomac, he recovered only as it closed. He then tried an adventure in raising cotton in the South, followed by another in oil wells in the West, both unfortunate; and it was not until after these failures that he entered the firm where he laid the solid foundation for the fortune and public philanthropy that made him the first citizen of his city. William James in youth essayed to be an artist, then went through the Medical School, but never practiced medicine or made any notable success in medical science. It was not until the age of forty-eight that he achieved a reputation by his work on psychology, a subject in which he had gradually become deeply interested. From this he was led to philosophy, and at his death no living philosopher had greater fame than he.

Examples of this kind might be multiplied indefinitely, but these are enough for our purpose. Some of them are cases where the early failures were in the same field in which success was afterwards attained; others were cases where the final triumph was in a subject quite different from that of the early efforts. In some of them the obstacles came from outside; in others from a false start in the wrong direction. In all the end was a notable contribution to the world. Probably each of these men would, throughout his life, have marked as disappointments many lesser things besides the obvious ones that have been here observed. To the ambitious in the best sense of the term, it often seems that life is an unending series of failures which in the total sum make up success. The higher the goal a man sets before himself the more frequently will he fall short of its attainment, and feel that he has failed when in fact he has accomplished much.

I have said that so long as a man lives he has not failed

unless he believes that he has failed, and sometimes he has not failed even then. Among the great prophets, reformers, and leaders of mankind some have died thinking that their labors had been in vain, their mission a failure, or their cause lost, when in fact after their death their work has borne abundant fruit from generation to generation. If this is true of them it is no less true of countless others unknown to fame, but, by the good they have done, shining in God's firmament as the stars forever. There has never been a failure greater than to his disciples Christ's appeared to be on Calvary. They thought it had been he who should have redeemed Israel, but at the time they took all for lost. In St. John's gospel the very last account of Christ's appearance opens with a failure that was a prelude to something far beyond any success hoped for. Seven of the disciples, not knowing what to do, returned to their former occupation as fishermen. They went forth, entered into a ship, and spent the whole night casting their nets. That night, we are told, they caught nothing, "but when the morning was now come, Jesus stood on the shore."

June 15, 1924

And he said unto them, When I sent you without purse, and scrip, and shoes, lacked ye any thing? And they said, Nothing. Then said he unto them, But now, he that hath a purse, let him take it, and likewise his scrip: and he that hath no sword, let him sell his garment, and buy one.

LUKE 22:35, 36.

According to St. Luke this was Christ's last direction to his disciples before his death, and it is certainly a very strange one. He could not have intended that they should use their weapons in resisting the attempt to seize him which was soon to take place, for he was about to demonstrate by his death that his mission was not to set up a temporal kingdom; and that same night he rebuked Peter for using his sword, and healed the servant's ear.

Was this direction actual or figurative? It may well have been both. It may have had some reference to the conditions that prevailed, but the interest to us lies in its figurative sense. We may suppose that he meant to warn his disciples that they were not to live a life of seclusion, withdrawn in contemplation from other people, but to move in the world of men. "I pray not," he said, "that Thou shouldst take them out of the world, but that Thou shouldst keep them from the evil." Since his doctrines were to be preached to all men, his followers were not to be confined to the profession of holy men in the East, set apart for ascetic lives, or even for teaching a small band of devotees. They were to preach to all men of whatever kind, station, or craft who were willing to make religion their motive power in life.

Religious contemplation has its place in deepening the

tone of thought and feeling, a place often too little regarded in the whirring tumult of our crowded lives. But it is not all. Almost everyone has an instinctive sympathy with the legend of St. Christopher. When that giant determined to serve Christ they set him at prayer and fasting, but he soon found himself unfitted by nature for a life of that kind, and longed to serve in a more active way. The monks, perceiving that he had no capacity for being saintly, sought to use his huge physical strength for manual labor, and set him to carry the pilgrims over a ford in the neighboring stream. One dark night a little child came to the ford anxious to cross. Christopher lifted him upon his broad shoulders, but found him marvelously heavy, and as the weight grew more and more he almost despaired of reaching the other bank, but he staggered on, and when he gained the farther shore he found his burden was the Christ Child, and he stands in legend forevermore as the saint who, meaning to bear the least of his brethren, bore Christ.

The much abused Puritans founded this College only ten years after they settled at Boston, and they did it, we are told in the quotation carved yonder upon the Johnston Gate, in order to train ministers, but from the first they educated here men who were to pursue all careers. Their principle that every act has a moral value was right; although, like other men whose practices were more ascetic than their neighbors, they exaggerated the negative side, and it is that side which has drawn the chief attention of posterity. No doubt they believed in letting your light so shine before men that they may see your good works, a text specially used in modern churches to stimulate giving money when a collection is taken. But it means far more than that and applies properly to the whole conduct of life.

The difference between the more or less highly civilized peoples does not depend upon the men specially set apart for holy lives. These may be found in large numbers among any people with a profound religious conviction, leading lives of the most rigorous devotion and self-denial, and often of spiritual exaltation. They are plentiful among the Moslems and the Hindus. Nor does the difference lie in the conscientious performance of religious duties by the mass of the faithful. No one can have witnessed an evening service in Saint Sophia in the days of the Sultan, or seen a hungry and thirsty group of men in the month of Ramadan, who had had neither food nor water since sunrise, waiting until the sun should set, or read of the devotions of the Arab in the desert, without knowing that the Mohammedan takes his religious observances far more seriously than the Christian in western lands.

The difference between the more or less highly progressive peoples is found rather in the fact that men pursuing secular occupations are more positively devoted thereto. The physicians are not only humanitarian, but earnest seekers in medical science; the lawyers are not only upright, but learned; the judges are not only impartial, but vigilant in ascertaining the law and the facts; the teachers are not only devoted, but well taught; the engineers are not only faithful, but highly competent; the men of affairs are not only honest, but enterprising; and so on through the whole range of professions and careers.

But someone will ask what this has to do with religion or morals, seeing that the motive is competition. Much every way. In the first place religion and morals, like everything else, are competitive; that is, they are refreshed and strengthened by example. Like other emotions they are contagious; and any of their results that are admired stir others to emulation. The mere fact, therefore, that a product of civilization is primarily caused by competition does not prove that its ultimate basis is not moral. Moreover, it is hard to contemplate the vast complex organization of the modern world and believe that it is built up and held together only by purely selfish and materialistic motives. During and since the great war we have learned something, if we did not know it before, about the nervous structure of human society. We have learned that it is based on mutual confidence, which in business we call credit; and this means a confidence that as a rule other people will fulfill their obligations, or in other words will do their duty. If that confidence were to disappear generally among men our civilization would crumble into fragments, and the most prosperous regions of the earth would be unable to support more than a fraction of their present population. In the bewilderment and loss of mutual confidence that has followed a political overturn in some places we have beheld people starving where food should have been abundant.

Could men have confidence that others would fulfill their obligations and do their duty, if they had no intention of doing so themselves? Clearly not. Most men intend to do their duty in accord with the standards of the civilization to which they belong, not from fear of bankruptcy or prison, but because it is their duty. They are faithful because they assume that right, as they understand it, is right, and wrong is wrong; because they are moral beings with moral motives; and this is an outward and visible sign of an inward and spiritual sense, whatever their religious philosophy may be. They have confidence that others will also do their duty by reason of ascribing to others the motives they themselves possess. We are therefore justified in maintaining that our civilization, with all its materialism, with all its sordid aspects, with all its hypocrisy, is ultimately based on its moral and religious principles, and that its defects are due to moral imperfections.

Let us go a step farther. If the religion or morality of a highly civilized people is better than that of a less progressive one it is not that they believe in it more earnestly, that they are more self-sacrificing for its sake, but that it is more fruitful because it has a wider scope, a larger outlook, and affects a greater part of life. It should cover the whole range of human possibilities, and transfigure every profession, every career, every occupation, every relation into which men enter. We live in a workaday world, and for most men the chief means of doing good lies in their daily toil.

In saying this let me not be understood as depreciating in the slightest direct philanthropic and social work; and public affairs, when the public interest is put above personal or party success. These are also positive duties, and fortunate, as well as worthy of the highest gratitude, are those who devote much energy thereto. To the man burdened with the cares and worries of his career they open fresh views of life, broaden his outlook, quicken his sympathies and enable him, while lightening the load of others, to estimate more justly his own. But they are not the only form of righteous conduct, in contrast with laboring for the unrighteous mammon; and they must not be regarded as the good deed that leavens or redeems the selfish business of breadwinning.

Anyone who looks upon his regular occupation as mere breadwinning has missed altogether its moral import. Less often fortunately than in the past, but still I fear not infrequently, young men say to themselves "I must do something to support myself, but I wish I were not obliged to do so." Such an idea, if not immoral, is unmoral, and falls far short of a true sense of moral duty. Those who by reason of illness cannot work we pity; those who can labor in God's vineyard but do not should be pitied even more, for moral is more lamentable than physical weakness. Good men must not only abstain from wrongdoing but be productive.

Every year at this season thousands of young men go forth from our colleges to seek their fortunes in the world, or let us say in the vineyard — it is the same thing. Thirty or forty years afterward they come back to celebrate the anniversary of their graduation. We will not ask them what they have done; the most modest of them might not tell us the truth, or perhaps some of the others either. We will ask the recording angels who come with them although they know it not; and we will not ask about those most conspicuous in men's eyes, for their careers are public. Here is a physician. His recording angel says that he began by selling his garment to buy the best equipment in medical science he could procure, and has always kept it bright by keeping up with the fast accumulating knowledge of his art. He has practiced in a small town where by his skill he has saved many lives that but for him would have flickered out, has dried many tears, and prevented untold suffering. His step along the corridor of the hospital, or on the threshold of the house, has brought hope, and when he entered his presence has been a benediction. Then comes a lawyer whose angel says that after a thorough study of his profession he took up practice in the same town, and quickly by his character, his sound knowledge, and good judgment earned the respect of his fellow citizens. Judges and juries have trusted his integrity which was a terror to the dishonest and the sly. Clients have relied implicitly upon his counsel. Men have sought him as an arbitrator in their disputes, and his uprightness has raised the general respect for law and justice. For a generation the moral tone of this town has been enlarged because these two men practiced their professions here. Another member of the class is an engineer. All his life he has been in the service of a large corporation, and, although he has never attained national fame, his angel records that his work has been both thorough and progressive. No accidents have ever occurred through mistakes in his construction, and his devices have greatly improved the service and the safety for the public. Few among them know how much they owe to him. His classmates do not know, but it is none the less for that. Among the crowd is a manufacturer, not at the head of a vast national trust, but a smaller factory of useful things. His angel says that his products are good; that their quality has raised the standard in the trade; that he has been fair to his competitors, to his customers and his workmen; that his factory has made his community prosperous and happy. He has been a father to the people there and made it a home of the best traditions of American life. There is a teacher, who would gladly learn and gladly teach. For years he has been at the head of a large school where his influence has radiated among the boys as noiseless as the beams of the spring sun on a garden. Year after year they have been stronger and better because he was there. Anything thereafter grafted upon the stock he had raised grew mightily because of the vigor he had given it. Of him the recording angel has no need to speak.

A good man can do untold good through his profession. Anyone who pursues his calling to the best of his ability, with a large view to its ultimate results, thereby serves and raises greatly the whole community, for the common road of men rightly traveled is the highway of the Eternal King.

June 14, 1925

The sun shall not smite thee by day, nor the moon by night.
PSALM 121:6.

THE PSALMIST promised to the faithful freedom from both sunstroke and moonstroke. The meaning of the first of these is clear — especially in the hot climate where the psalm was written. But to most people at the present day the second promise is either meaningless, or a reminder of an ancient and obsolete superstition that the shining of the moon on the face during sleep will cause insanity — a superstition still preserved in our word lunatic.

Although we have long ceased to believe that the

moon has any connection with mental disease, the intent of the benediction is as vital as ever. In present day prose, it might be expressed thus: "You shall be free from illness in body or aberration in mind," and of these the second is the more important to the man himself, and of by far the greater moment to the rest of the world. If to err in thought is an evil, and to escape it a benefit to oneself and others, there is also a duty to keep one's mind from error and to think aright.

We say that public opinion rules the world, and we often say so carelessly, because by public opinion we are apt to mean merely the ideas held by ourselves and the little group of people to which we belong. Nevertheless it is true that public opinion does rule. The slave trade was abolished by it, and so later was slavery — although in this case not without a struggle. Taking the civilized world over, corruption in public life, while not, indeed, abolished, has been greatly reduced in the last two hundred years by the force of public opinion; and this has occurred not so much from a perception that corruption is practiced at the cost of the whole community, but chiefly from a sense of its inherent iniquity. Cruel forms of punishment for crime, torture in obtaining evidence, have disappeared in the same period under the pressure of this compelling influence. In short, the advance of civilization in its social and moral conditions is caused and measured by the progress of opinion.

Public opinion is, therefore, of the highest consequence to mankind. But, after all, the stuff it is made of is only the opinions of individuals combined into a mass. In its formation some men count for more than others, but everyone counts for something; and most men count for more than they are aware. We are much too inclined to think that hasty judgments, idle words, careless statements of passing impressions are unimportant; and yet these may have a distinct influence on whoever hears them. Everyone truly counts to some extent, for although many people form no opinions of their own and merely reflect their surroundings — Laodiceans, neither hot nor cold — spineless drifters without self-direction — still they have an effect, and may both prevent the spread of right-thought, and promote a mischievous course. They are a shifting cargo in the ship of state, a peril if the bulkheads break.

All this is true, not only of opinions about public matters, but also about what is right, just, honorable, and generous in personal conduct. As a rule, indeed, public morals are built upon private morals, and a stable commonwealth does not stand upon an unsound moral foundation. Let us repeat, therefore, that morals, public and private, depend upon opinion. The morality of a people is sustained by a general opinion of its rightfulness, and a general condemnation of its violation. All men sometimes do, and a few men often do, what they know to be wrong; but even so they usually try to justify to themselves, or at least to palliate, their sins. In the main men conduct themselves, both in public and private life, in accordance with their moral opinions, or the opinions of those they respect, or the opinions prevalent among the people with whom they mix. If so, right opinions are of supreme importance, and the duty of holding right opinions is one of paramount obligation.

This does not mean that all true men should think

alike. Men differ, must differ, and ought to differ; but that does not affect the momentous results of wrong opinions, or the imperative duty of thinking right. Nor is it any excuse that other people think the same. It is quite as bad, and often worse, to think wrong with the majority as to be in the wrong alone. If truth were so easy to ascertain that all honest-minded people instinctively thought alike, the duty to think right would involve too little effort to need an exhortation. Life is so complex in its personal, social, public, and international relations, it has so many facets, refracts the light in so many different ways, that it is very difficult to see it aright, or to take into account in due proportion all the manifold elements it contains.

We must strive to see as much as we can, to keep our minds as clear from error as possible, and form our judgments by earnest, painstaking effort. We must beware of assuming that an idea is true because it is old or because it is new, but try simply to discover whether it is true or not. To put the matter more accurately, we must endeavor to ascertain how much of truth or error it contains; for from history we learn that the common mistake of men has been to assume that of two opposing views one is absolutely right and the other wholly wrong, when in fact each had a savor of truth confused by exaggeration and error. From this cause have flowed political and religious struggles, resulting indeed in progress, but progress less complete and less durable than might have come from earnest effort on both sides to seek for what was right in each. In such cases the elements of truth on each side were not brought face to face and weighed in the balance; but men have weighed what truth there was on their own side against the errors on the other. To see clearly one's own modicum of truth and what is wrong in one's opponents is an easy way of forming a judgment, but not a method that leads either to truth or to harmony.

It is often thought that the best means of promoting the search for truth is to have men advocate divergent views as strongly as they can, with the idea that from the discord truth will emerge. This has its merit in assuring that no grain of truth will remain obscure; and it is excellent when, as in a court, there are judges and jurors entrusted with the duty of remaining impartial and forming a right judgment. But in his part in creating opinion a citizen is both advocate and judge. Not only does he present his views, but he contributes also to the public judgment; and therefore he should strive for the nearest approximation he can make to truth. Moreover, by so doing he becomes a larger force. It was Lincoln rather than Garrison or Phillips that convinced his people of the necessity for emancipation.

There are times of stress when men must fight for the greater truth as they see it against another aspect of truth which in the insistent strife is less vital; times when duty demands not to ask the reason why, but to do and die. Then duty becomes heroic, but intellectually simple. In more tranquil periods the supreme duty is to think aright. It is then that opinions can, and should, be formed that will direct action when the stress comes. Let us not forget that in peace the conflicting opinions are formed that later produce wars; that in quiet times the social ideas grow which, if erroneous, collect the explosives for subsequent catastrophes. It is then that the duty is incumbent to form, and help others to form, correct, unbiased opinions, particularly upon those subjects in which we may have special means of reaching a right judgment.

Before we were drawn into the war, and still more since, we have heard much of the need of preparedness, and rightly so. But preparation should not be merely of material things, but of opinions. Most of all we need thinking to prepare for crises ahead. In fact there was never more need of forethought than now, for the public men of the present day are, as a rule, apt to take short views. For meeting such a need educated men, and among them college graduates, are peculiarly responsible, because they have been furnished above others with the means of forming opinions by ascertaining the facts on which they should be based, and by considering them from an abstract, and hence a detached, point of view. Such men are in a real sense the watchmen of the people, for if they see the evil coming and give not warning, the blood of the people who suffer should be required at their hand; and not less should it be required when they have failed to see the evil after receiving the privilege of education that should have given them the power of seeing.

Wrong opinions come mainly from lack of sight, from not seeing far enough, or widely enough, or from obstacles in the line of vision, and therefore from failing to take into account a part of the factors in the problem. Such nearsightedness, or defective vision, is due partly to our ignorance — in large part unavoidable because we know, and can know, only a small portion of the infinite compass of eternal truth. It is partly due also to the narrowness of our sympathies which prevents us from comprehending the sentiments and point of view of others, who are quite as sincere, intelligent, and well informed as ourselves, perhaps familiar with aspects of the matter we know little about, and gifted with a deeper insight. It is due in no small measure to prejudice which obscures our vision — usually quite unconsciously to ourselves, for prejudice that is conscious, like a mist at the rising of the sun, is likely to be about to dissipate. And herein lies one of the great difficulties in thinking aright, that we do not know when we are wrong, or we should not be wrong. The man who knows the right trail does not miss it. We go wrong because the moon has smitten our minds with error.

Again our failure to see clearly is due partly to passion that blinds us — often selfish, ignoble passion, impatience with those who oppose us, jealousy, vindictiveness, fear, or avarice of wealth or fame. Sometimes the passion springs from better motives, a desire to help others unjustly treated, or eagerness for the success of a cause in whose righteousness we have faith. I knew a man who made a rule when indignant to write a letter as strongly as he felt, then address it to himself, and drop it into the mail. On receiving it the next morning he had an impression of the way it would affect the person for whom it was intended. Not a bad thing to do, if not literally, at least in imagination, as a means of putting oneself in another's place.

The fact is that over all these sources of shortsightedness we have some control, over many of them very great control. We can lessen our ignorance by earnest search for truth. We can widen our sympathies, and reduce our prejudice by striving to do so, and that without letting our resolution be sicklied o'er by the pale cast of thought.

We can control our passions by frankly acknowledging their existence to ourselves.

Above all, we can place ourselves on a higher plane of vision by striving to look at things from a loftier standpoint. We can endeavor to rise above our own sentiments, surroundings, and purposes until they assume their true proportions in a wider horizon. We can try to think how they would be regarded by a Being infinite in knowledge, in love, and in sympathy with all sentient creatures that now are, or hereafter will be, living upon the earth. No doubt we shall still be in error, because we are finite, severely limited in mind and heart; but the nearest approach we can make to the pure white light of truth is to raise our thoughts as closely as we are able to those of the Infinite and Eternal.

June 20, 1926

The earth is the Lord's, and the fulness thereof; the world, and they that dwell therein.
For he hath founded it upon the seas, and established it upon the floods.   PSALM 24:1, 2.

WE SHOULD expect "for he hath founded it upon a rock" but instead it is said to be founded upon the floods.

The sea is ever changing with calm and storm; over a large part of the globe it is rarely for many days the same. At times it is quiet, beautiful, and beneficent, at others fierce, violent, terrific; and yet it is the same sea that the first sailor looked upon. The Mediterranean that Homer's heroes traversed is the Mediterranean of St.

Paul's voyage, of the Venetian, Genoese, and Turkish galleys, and of excursionists today. To Leif Ericson the north Atlantic presented the same appearance that it does still, and the track of Columbus looks now as it did when he made his great adventure.

But the Gaul of Caesar's time would hardly recognize modern France as his native land; the ancient inhabitant of the West Riding of Yorkshire, or of Westphalia, would find little that is familiar in the present landscape. Man has worked his will upon the land. He has cut down the forests, drained the marshes, planted fields of grain, covered the country with a network of roads, railroads, and bridges, and built upon it cities, until he has quite changed the face of nature. But the sea he cannot alter; it remains forever changing, yet eternally the same.

The mind of man is like the sea; for man's thought is ever shifting, and yet from the earliest written records human nature has been much like what it is today. Were it not so, ancient history and literature would not have for us the attraction and the value they possess. They would seem strange and distant tales of unfamiliar beings. But, in fact, despite new ideas and principles that have since prevailed, we recognize at once among the Israelites, among the prominent figures of Greek and Roman history, the strong and the weak, the wise and the foolish, the good and the ignoble characters. What is more, the relatively simple conditions of those times enable us to see these qualities even more readily than when we try to analyze the conduct of men who live in our more complex modern life. The problems of good and evil, of character and of duty, remain eternally the same; but their application to the conduct of life presents an endless variety of new questions, because these arise in a constantly shifting environment; and with the vast increase in control over the powers of nature the changes in man's condition now come far more rapidly than ever before. Therefore the chief object of the College is not to send forth her sons armed to grapple with the immediate problems of the present day, but rather those that will arise hereafter, for we know that when these men have reached a position to influence their solution, the problems will no longer be the same. In the warfare with the submarines a streak of bubbles revealed the rush of a torpedo under water, but the missile was not where the foremost bubbles broke. It had already gone yards ahead; and so in all things the cause is far in advance of the symptoms that betray it. New causes are at work and will manifest themselves hereafter, for which men must be prepared. For that reason we do not seek to provide our students with ready-made solutions for current questions, but to make them resourceful in themselves by equipping them with the capacity to solve problems yet unknown, whose nature cannot now be conjectured.

Men do not sail the same old ocean with the craft of long ago. We do not, like our ancestors, lay our course for a distant port by working to the right latitude and sailing on that parallel until a landfall is made. We do not even depend upon the magnetic compass and the chronometer, but on a gyroscopic compass, and on correct time flashed out by radio from Greenwich or Washington. Nor are soundings taken by the old methods; and yet with better means the art of navigation still depends upon calculating our true position by the sun and stars.

Mankind is ever thinking it has attained the truth, until

a later generation finds that what had been discovered was but partly true. Lavoisier in the eighteenth century made a vast advance by proclaiming the conservation of matter. In its solid form the particles were believed to be in close contact; and chemical science found in the atoms the ultimate indivisible particles of matter arranged in a series of elements. But now we are told that these are divisible, probably to some extent transmutable, and, instead of being solid, composed of minute electrons, moving rapidly within an open space. If so, there may be nothing solid in the sense in which it was formerly conceived, while matter and energy, instead of being wholly distinct, may be both different phenomena of force.

Of one thing we may be sure, that whatever we know of nature today will not prove to be wholly correct hereafter. Men will discover new truth of which we now know only a part, and thus they will move on to larger and more perfect thought. Not in science alone, but in all other kinds of knowledge man progresses by a series of approximations, not exact, but tending to bring him nearer to the truth. To stop would be his ruin. If life were not a constant effort man's powers would atrophy. Constant change demands ceaseless activity, and activity is the price of vigor. If it were not so man would be at the end of his quest, his advance would cease, his power of will and thought decline. He must work on toward an endless goal, knowing that at infinity alone is truth complete.

We live in an age when knowledge has increased, when our conceptions have enlarged with unprecedented speed; and this has caused confusion of thought, and fresh difficulties in adjustment. The power over natural forces has made the difference between the material conditions of human life today and a century and a half ago greater than the difference between the conditions at that time and at the birth of Christ. No wonder we speak of our time as one of transition, that some men cling to that which has been familiar, skeptical about the new; while others tend to discredit the past, assuming in each generation, as a friend of mine once put it, that human reason began about thirty years ago. Both look on opposite sides of a shield whereof neither sees the whole.

The art of life lies largely in distinguishing the eddy from the stream. There is a current in human destiny that bears the world onwards, not always in the same direction, but in spite of eddies, and turns and shallows not without a continuity. The wise man, the earnest man, the man of courage and convictions, strives while living in the present to live for something more; to see an ultimate object in his life's work in harmony with a larger purpose; and to learn from the past a wisdom that will enable him to pierce the mists of the future.

The difficulty, the uncertainty, in applying eternal principles to new conditions causes good men, eagerly seeking the same end, to differ profoundly about the means to be employed; and they are prone to attribute to each other a larger influence from self-interest than is quite just. More is often due to personal association and experience than to conscious selfishness, and usually neither opponent is altogether right or wrong. William James remarked that Harvard men could be found on the wrong side of every question; and that is no doubt true in the eyes of any man with decided opinions; but we may assume he did not mean that on every question there are Harvard graduates deliberately supporting the side they believe to be wrong. It is both generous and sensible to assume the honesty of an opponent. Save in the case where a choice among men has to be made, the thing to be opposed is a wrong principle, idea, or attitude, not the individual who is its advocate. To argue not the principle involved, but the personal character or conduct of an antagonist, is both bad logic and bad morals. It is dragging a red herring across the trail, instead of pursuing the search for truth. Often it is done from lack of clear thinking, but not seldom from temper, or an attempt to obscure the issue. In the heat of controversy we are apt to forget that a wholly insincere man is rarely very dangerous. The important thing in the questions we are called upon to meet, whether controversial or not, whether in public affairs, in a profession, or in business, is faith that what we are ourselves striving to do is worth doing, and that we are doing it by methods whose integrity will bear the test of time.

If, in reading the pages of history or romance, any man would rather have been a character that he admires than one that he contemns, let him be so now. Nor in this matter is it of consequence whether his deeds, or his name, will be publicly remembered or not. The lives worth living are not only those recorded. The figures so celebrated are few, and in part accidental. Most of their good work could not have been done without the support of many whose names have not survived the erosion of time. The progress of great peoples is due to countless citizens, clear in their judgment on the problems they are called upon to meet, firm in their conception of duty, strong in their faith that forever right is right and wrong is wrong, and steadfast wherever fate may lead in fair weather or foul. Therefore when you have done good be not overanxious that it be known. Not seldom there is difficulty in accomplishing much and getting the credit for it. The essential is the good done; the credit is a by-product, which may, or may not, follow, and desire therefor often impedes the work itself. It is a worthy ambition to desire to make in one's day and generation one's mark for good, great or small, obvious or unknown, material or spiritual; one cannot, indeed, understand how any man can be content to end his life without contributing to the world more than he has received therefrom. But the desire is not enough, it must also be directed aright.

Progress and usefulness mean keeping abreast of new conditions, an unending adaptation to new environment, yet always with the same objective, the eternal quest for the true and just, the endless conflict with the ignoble and unworthy. Before the last member of this class shall pass away the world will be very different from what it is today, a better world if men now young shall strive to adjust its changes to the everlasting principles of righteousness.

June 19, 1927

What profit hath a man of all his labor which he taketh under the sun? ECCLESIASTES 1:3.

THE WRITER of this book, who speaks of himself as the Preacher and King in Jerusalem, took a depressing view of life. He examined all its phases, its pleasures, its labors, the possession of wealth and power, and found them all to be vanity and vexation of spirit. It is the old cry that has echoed down the ages, from philosophers with a clear, cold analysis, but without enthusiasm or conviction beyond the range of palpable conditions.

Young men starting out on their careers, eager for action, with life and its ventures before them, may well avoid disappointment by asking themselves what profit a man hath of all his labor that he taketh under the sun; what, if any, the nature of that profit may be, and how, if worth having, it may be obtained.

For the great mass of men engaged in manual and mechanical labor there seems a tendency to revert to the old conception associated with the story of Adam's expulsion from the Garden of Eden — namely that his sin forced upon him the curse of work, obliging him to earn bread only by the sweat of his face. There is no use in arguing that labor is not a curse by showing that civilization has advanced where work has been necessary to maintain life; for the fact remains that a great many people regard labor as an unfortunate evil. No doubt the monotony of many specialized factory tasks has had this result; for each workman does not create his own complete product, and hence cannot take the same pride and pleasure in it as in the simpler times of personal, skilled crafts. Nor has the spirit of team play brought as yet a new spirit to replace the motive that has gone. Still I see much manual labor in which men can, and I believe do, take interest and pride.

But I do not want to discuss a class of labor whereof I have too little knowledge to speak with wisdom. The men graduating here will do work in which they certainly can take pride, and, if regarded aright, should take pleasure. But again we may ask ourselves with the Preacher, what doth it profit? Is it because it is remunerative and brings wealth? Often it does, and with many of you it will. But does a man's life consist in the multitude of things that he possesses? Do large houses, sumptuous meals, a retinue of servants, garages full of high-priced automobiles, suffice to make life happy?

General Charles R. Lowell, a few days before his death in the battle of Cedar Creek, wrote to his friend Major Henry L. Higginson "Don't grow rich; if you once begin, you will find it much more difficult to be a useful citizen. The useful citizen is a mighty inconspicuous hero." After several false starts Major Higginson did grow rich, but it was very far in his case from making useful citizenship difficult. In fact, it distinctly helped his usefulness, and for some years before his death he was commonly regarded as the first citizen of his native city. Wealth may be a means to an end, but beware of making it an end in itself. The man who so regards it, who sets his heart solely on accumulating it, is termed a miser, and such a one is proverbially a stunted, unhappy being. Nor is he who spends it in an attempt to gratify his selfish ambition much better off. Rich men have been good and bad, happy and miserable. The real criterion of its value is how it is used. Wealth may help or hamper a man in getting a start in life. Later it may be a source of strength, and thereby enlarge a man's opportunities for good or evil. In this it is like natural ability or education, or anything else that increases one's power over the actions and thoughts of other men. None of these things in themselves make happiness or usefulness. That depends upon the purpose for which they are employed. If one treats all his potentials, mental and material, as aids in the accomplishment of a distant object, in accord with an overruling moral purpose, his own usefulness and happiness will be enveloped and safeguarded in something greater than himself. Wealth is merely a means to a farther end.

How about a profit in labor for its own sake? To some men work, and especially intellectual work, is in itself a pleasure; but almost any work that is really worth doing involves much drudgery, anxiety, and disappointment. If one's only object in labor is one's own satisfaction, the ordinary man will ask himself sadly whether he derives as much pleasure as pain from it, or in the words of the Preacher whether it is not vanity and vexation of spirit. But if he regards it as a means to a greater end, it changes its aspect and glows with the promise of a coming light. Immediate personal success fades before the brighter object to which, however modestly, the work is contributing. Labor, then, draws its true dignity, its significance, and its gift of happiness from the vision of a farther end.

If, in the main, work and wealth contribute to happiness incidentally, why not strive for happiness directly? Why not seek at least the higher and innocent pleasures of life as we may? This the Preacher rightly denounces as vanity and vexation of spirit. A search for happiness is, for the result obtained, the most barren chase in which a man with any depth of nature can engage. Happiness is a by-product of life. Many a man, who has spent his time in leisure, longs in middle life to take up something that he feels to be worth while. Fortunately, respectable indolence, or passing one's whole time in harmless amusements, is not a serious temptation at the present day. We live in an age of almost feverish activity. Men want to do something, to count for something; and that is true both in youth and in advancing years. Formerly men retired from a business or profession in middle life to devote themselves to literature and leisure. A merchant in Boston a century ago wrote a letter to his father on that gentleman's fifty-sixth birthday, suggesting that there was no need for both of them in the counting house. His father took the hint and came regularly to the office no more. That would hardly be a safe letter for a son to write to his father in these more busy times.

At the other end of the scale, and perhaps partly by reason of this very thirst for action, the ascetic, who shuns all enjoyment on principle, has also disappeared. Because we reject pleasure as an end it is not wise to reject recreation and pleasure as a means. The ascetic who avoids a thing because he enjoys it is like the English Puritans of whom Macaulay said that they condemned bear-baiting, not because it gave pain to the bear, but because it gave pleasure to the spectators. Pleasure, like work and wealth, is by itself vanity and may become mere vexation of spirit; but he who enjoys recreation, who cherishes an avocation in which he delights, strengthens his spirit for a harder task. A wise friend of mine remarked that those who in the stress of life work hard usually play hard also. Such men drink of the brook in their way and lift up their heads. The secret again is looking to something beyond.

Vanity of vanities, cried the Preacher, all is vanity and vexation of spirit. "I said in mine heart. Go to now, I will prove thee with mirth, therefore enjoy pleasure: and, behold, this also is vanity.... I hated life; because the work that is wrought under the sun is grievous unto me: for all is vanity and vexation of spirit. Yea, I hated all my labour which I had taken under the sun.... Wherefore I praised the dead which are already dead more than the living which are yet alive." Is work only the monotonous trample of the treadmill, pleasure and joy the chasing of shapes that vanish at the touch, the tasting of fruits that turn to ashes on the palate? To morbid temperaments that look no farther than the things themselves this may seem true — and most men have a seam of pathos running beneath their nature which at times crops up and makes them morbid. But when we look beyond the work itself the scene appears to change.

If we should awake some morning with a conviction that the world would end tomorrow we should all lay down our tools and wait. Of what use to finish that building or that book, that plan for a commercial enterprise or foreign travel, or to pursue those reveries of entering a business or a profession? How many men would start eagerly on the study of law or medicine if they knew they would die the day their training was over? How fully would the zest depart from our work in life if we believed that as soon as we were gone it would be effaced as fully as if we had never lived and wrought? We enjoy our work because we feel that it is worth doing, and it is worth doing because in some form it will endure. It has a moral value that outlasts the hour in which it is done and the man who does it.

Everything we know has been affected by some cause, and affects everything that will come to pass hereafter. No act, good or evil, is wholly without influence upon the future, impossible as it may be to trace the sequence. The civilization we inherit is due not alone to great figures of the past whose fame has been perpetuated, but also to numberless men and women, unknown, but with principles, courage, and endurance, who have slowly built up standards by which we live.

Since every act has consequences which may be more momentous than in our blindness we imagine, since every act must certainly conduce toward an ultimate result, and therefore is a means toward an end, it behooves a man to ask himself what in his case that end shall be. Many of the hard problems of life are rendered less impenetrable by looking beyond them to a more distant object. Much of the dissension in the world, much of the error, of the distorted values, of the mischievous lack of a sense of proportion, come from mistaking means for ends, from regarding a proximate end as final.

That one is working for an end outside and above oneself, that one's labor contributes to a lofty purpose, is what makes it, and with it life itself, worth while; and the more distant the end the grander the prospect. The moral qualities are not only real, but with the growth of civilization they tend to expand. In its early stages the ties that bound men together were restricted to the family or the tribe. Everyone beyond was, if not presumptively an enemy, at least a stranger who had no claim to consideration. Then larger and larger groups were formed, sympathy and the sense of duty enlarged still more rapidly, until today the best of men feel that all mankind are one fellowship and that every creature capable of suffering is entitled to human sympathy. It is the same of the purpose of our strivings. Confined at first to small groups of neighbors and a narrow range of thought, it widens its horizon and extends its scope. If it be true that to be worthy our object must lie outside ourselves, it is not less true that the more distant and the more inclusive it is the more its pursuit is worth while.

There remains no place for vanity and vexation of spirit, save in our own lack of sight. A man starts in the morning of life's journey with the distant peak shining white and clear in the beams of the rising sun. Winds spring up and the clouds gather about the summit, slowly dropping down the sides until they lie thickly around the base. He can see the guiding peak no more; but does he think that it has gone? He has learned the way. Let him follow it until his feet reach the ascending slopes. The man who has no sense of a landmark when he loses sight of it will lose his way; and he that sees no purpose in his conduct beyond his own pleasures and desires has no philosophy, or only a hedonistic one that shrinks from his grasp when he tries to seize it. A philosophy with an object outside of oneself is an essential in all religion, and a complete philosophy is one that ends in a harmony of all things.

Vastly as knowledge has increased, it is still far from perfect. We have not yet learned to weigh imponderables; though we can work with them, and in much of human life they are the most important elements. Every little while we are finding something about the physical forces which shows that the laws we have been taught are not exact. But even where accuracy has been attained they do not explain the phenomena of life. So far as we can ascertain, no doubt, all the complex processes of life follow precisely the laws of physics and of chemistry. Nothing takes place in the tissues of any plant or animal contrary to those laws, and yet they do not account for all that happens. The biologist appears on the scene, and explains how these complex reactions of living tissues are due to the existence of life. They are all in accord with physical laws, but life determines the conditions under which those laws shall operate. Without it living creatures would not be alive, be what they are, and behave as they do. Life is not a mere complex of intricate chemical reactions, although it involves them at every point. It is the same with moral forces. Emotions, sentiments, volitions, affections, and aspirations are real, and are not a mere manifestation of material reactions, though accompanied thereby. As life is a different thing from the chemistry it employs, so thought is distinct from the material basis on which it rests.

Man cannot set a limit to his thought. He cannot stop with the ancient legend that the world was held up in the arms of Hercules who stood upon a tortoise, without asking what supports the tortoise. While we discover electrons and germs too small for the microscope, and stars so far away that we measure their distance by the thousands of years it takes their light to travel to the earth, we can imagine these particles subdivided and stars still farther off. Man cannot conceive of a boundary to space, or a time that began or will end, because he cannot fetter the processes of his own mind. He cannot find a purpose so remote that it may not be more distant yet, and the farther away the object the more profound the joy of association therewith. Weak, dull, and blind as man is, he was made for infinite conceptions of which he is to partake. After describing the heavenly paradise with all the glory of his fervid imagination, Dante ends his poem with a blazing but still distant light that typified God himself. Only at infinity can the vision be finished and the end complete.

June 17, 1928

The light of the body is the eye: if therefore thine eye be single, thy whole body shall be full of light.
But if thine eye be evil, thy whole body shall be full of darkness. If therefore the light that is in thee be darkness, how great is that darkness! MATTHEW 6:22, 23.

RELIGIOUS literature and romance are filled with examples of the choice between good and evil. The good path is represented as hard, encompassed by temptations, requiring purpose and fortitude; but the decision to be made is on each occasion clear. Moral earnestness is required, yet the choice is between obvious right and wrong. Such a choice would be easy. In the maze of life, however, the conditions are much more insidious. The alternatives are by no means always a rugged but righteous road that winds upward, and a pleasant way leading surely to ultimate perdition. Often the paths do not seem very different, nor to diverge much; and a clear vision is required to see whither they tend. Fortunately, a wrong choice does not finally settle the destination, for there are byways to return to the true road, arduous, no doubt, but passable.

A simile or a parable may be pushed beyond its proper meaning, and hence one must not carry it too far. All I want to point out is that the important decisions in life are by no means always and evidently momentous at the time. The right and wrong of the choice may be clear but not the consequences involved, because they affect not so much the outward career of the actor as his own personal character. Some years ago two young men sailed a small boat, built on the south shore of Cape Cod, to the purchaser at Marblehead. As they rounded the Cape a thick fog came on, and thinking they might have to drop the anchor quickly in the night they brought it aft, with the rope fast, and lashed it on the quarter-deck by the cockpit. When morning came, and they could see somewhat through the haze, they found themselves off Minot's Ledge instead of Marblehead. The anchor on the quarter had caused a deviation of the compass in the cockpit; a result they had not foreseen. Of course no moral question was involved in this case, but it may illustrate what I mean. The compass is to the mariner what conscience is to a man. A deviation involves a wrong course. That is the significance in our text of the eye being single and the whole body full of light.

Conscience may suffer deviation in various ways. One of the most common is by small concessions to one's own inclinations, known not to be right, but not thought of much consequence and self-excused at the moment. Stevenson's tale of Dr. Jekyll and Mr. Hyde is popularly thought to be the well-worn fable of a struggle between a man's better and worse natures; but to me it has always seemed far more subtle. Dr. Jekyll was not the good part of the man. If it had been, it would no doubt have prevailed over the baser qualities. These would have appeared as they did finally in all their abhorrent reality, and the better part would have been shocked into rejecting them. But Dr. Jekyll was the whole man, with both higher and lower impulses. To the latter he yielded, turning himself for a time into Mr. Hyde, with a sly wink at his own cleverness. He did not think he was doing anything very bad, though he did not want to be found out, until at last the evil habit had been cultivated to such a strength that he could not resist it, and he was a permanent Hyde.

Call it searing the conscience, call it dimming the moral sight, call it what you will, the process, in greater or less degree, is not confined to fiction. Men have started in life with good intentions and ended reprobates. When the catastrophe comes in such cases, when, for example, an embezzlement is discovered, a long series of gradually increasing malversations appear, beginning with intent to replace, and ending in desperation. All along a series, also, of excuses until the edge of the conscience has become dulled. The end was not willed from the beginning; there was no deliberate choice between honesty and a life of crime. One step led to another, as with Dr. Jekyll, and till near the close the true state of affairs was not perceived. That this is true is evident from the fact that the defaulter sometimes continues to hold a respected position, or even to be an active church member. This is certainly not always and from the outset conscious hypocrisy. There is at times a growing blindness of the soul, and when the light of such a man is darkness, how great is that darkness.

On purpose I have sketched an extreme and somber picture of trifling with the eye that started single; but in lesser degree every man must jealously guard his vision lest he fall short of the highest character that he would reach; for a dimness of the moral sight, a blunting of the keen edge of sensibility, is the most insidious of perils. This, I think, is what Phillips Brooks meant in a sermon I heard him preach half a century ago, when he spoke of the difference between a man's falling within his resolution and outside of it. The former was a conscious fault, recognized by the man as such, for which he was sorry, and resolved not to commit again; the latter an excused fault, condoned by himself, and therefore likely to be repeated. Such a fault may be small, but small faults gradually dim the sight. Well did the Old Testament singer exclaim, "Take us the foxes, the little foxes that spoil the vines."

June 16, 1929

> *And it shall be, when the Lord thy God shall have brought thee into the land which he sware unto thy fathers, . . . vineyards and olive trees, which thou plantedst not: when thou shalt have eaten and be full;*
>
> *Then, beware lest thou forget the Lord, which brought thee forth out of the land of Egypt, from the house of bondage.*
>
> DEUTERONOMY 6:10–12.

NEXT year we shall celebrate the third centenary of the settlement of Boston, and six years later, that of the foundation of Harvard College. Preparations are now being made for those events. It is natural, therefore, to survey a part of that period — not an insignificant one in recent human history — and, perhaps, a comparison of the condition prevailing in our country within the memory of men still active with what it is today may have a lesson for those who are about to take up the work of life. Fifty years ago, although our forebears had been on this continent two centuries and a half, although the United States had enjoyed political independence for a century, we were still in many intellectual ways an offshoot or satellite of Europe.

An inventive people on our own initiative we had certainly become. The telegraph, and very recently the telephone, had been produced here, likewise sewing and agricultural machines, and vulcanized rubber, the screw propeller — which incidentally made sailing vessels obsolescent — replaced wooden by steel hulls, and thereby in time destroyed our shipping industry. Within three miles of this place anaesthesia had first been applied in surgery, and a new era opened in operations. It is needless to say more, for volumes have been written on American invention, and they portray a vast service to mankind. Nevertheless, fifty years ago our intellectual leadership, including that in pure science, was coming to us mainly from abroad. Medical students, and indeed almost all others, save in law, went to Europe to complete their education, not because, as now, something may always be gained in a foreign land of high culture, but because our universities could not give a training comparable to that given by those of the old world, and especially those in Germany. In fact, apart from elementary textbooks and the subject of American history — which did not then have much interest for European scholars — most of the works used for higher education in this country were written by foreigners.

At that time there was, indeed, less intellectual independence of thought than at an earlier period. The literary galaxy of men born in the generation following our national independence was passing away, and their place was imperfectly supplied. In the early eighties Sir Henry Maine, by no means an unfriendly critic, in discussing the merits of our Constitution wrote:

> The power to grant patents by Federal authority has, however, made the American people the first in the world for the number and ingenuity of the inventions by which it has promoted the "useful arts"; while, on the other hand, the neglect to exercise this power for the advantage of foreign writers has condemned the whole American community to a literary servitude unparalleled in the history of thought.

Doubtless that was an exaggeration. Nevertheless it contained an element of truth, and expressed an opinion about our people not uncommon in Europe. One sees it in the neglect of military men there to study our Civil War. Had either Austrian or French generals learned the lessons taught in that war, the history of Germany and thereby of Europe might have been very different, for the battles of both Sadowa and Gravelotte might well have been defeats for the Germans. But a generation passed before the contributions to the art of war made by our great conflict were perceived in Europe. The cause to which Maine assigned what he called our servitude was no doubt superficial. A more serious reason lay in the fact that we were engaged in expanding over a vast continent, tilling its soil, opening its mines, creating its industries, and its means of transportation. The very growth of railroads, by making the western lands accessible, drained away energy that in a circumscribed community might have been turned into intellectual channels.

Partly from our own preoccupation in subduing a

wilderness, partly from an instinct for preserving our own identity, we maintained in political relations with Europe an attitude of aloofness; and no doubt rightly so, because in our remoteness, our comparative lack of power, the small respect in which we were held abroad, we could have little influence on world affairs, and a close political contact would have meant being drawn along in a current made by others and quite beyond our control.

Within the last half century great changes have taken place. The frontier, and with it the spirit of the frontiersman, disappeared. The great work of occupying the whole country was completed. Our land can support a much larger population, but the vast unpeopled West exists no longer. The national territory is not full but it is occupied, and we have been constrained to look outward. The Spanish War which, with its results in the annexation of the Philippines, forced us to be a great power in the Pacific, brought a change in our relations to other nations and made us partly conscious of the fact. In the meantime our own internal development of industry had been giving us a new position in the world. We have become a rich and powerful nation, potentially the richest and most powerful on the earth. The great war revealed this to foreign powers, and opened our own eyes to the new position we had acquired. We know it. We cannot ignore it. We should not try to conduct our affairs as though it were not true, and we must assume the responsibilities that it entails.

The rank that the United States has now attained is in part the work of our own people. The action of the Constitutional Convention at Philadelphia which decided that we should be one nation, with no internal customhouses, and a truly national government, made our development possible. The energy and foresight of our pioneers in industry, transportation, and agriculture carried us to the point we have reached. But beneath that lies the mineral wealth in iron, copper, coal, and oil, which we did not create, which has been given freely by the bounty of nature. Our forebears did not come because the land contained these vast sources of future wealth. They knew nothing of them, and, if they had, would probably not have valued them highly. In fact most of them lie so far from the Atlantic seaboard that the early settlers would doubtless have regarded them as quite beyond their reach. All the more from the fact that these bounties are fortuitous do they lay upon us a duty to use them so that all mankind may be the better because America is inhabited by Americans.

Obligations are also laid upon us by our very power and wealth. No man liveth to himself alone, nor does any nation. We cannot, by shutting our eyes or by a process of isolation, deceive ourselves about our duties to the rest of mankind. Nor have we really ever desired to do so; but we have not always appreciated that the magnitude of our trust has grown with our strength; that the great have greater opportunities; that all their acts have a more far-reaching effect, and entail therefore larger duties. The form this responsibility should take may well be a matter for discussion, but in some form we must not shirk it, and it lies especially upon the generation that is now coming onto the stage. I may add that it lies with peculiar weight upon the young men who are setting out with the equipment of a generous education; who in the words of Matthew Arnold have learned to see clear and think straight; for if the graduating class before me has not learned this art, it has not received the best the College has to give.

In the ancient world there were two states, not unlike in their material conditions. Both were maritime peoples with an extensive commerce and a powerful fleet. Both were conquered and annexed by the Romans. One of them, Athens, in matters intellectual overcame its conquerors, forcing Rome to copy the models created by her; and she has left to the world the greatest treasure in thought and art that any single state has ever had the privilege to bestow on posterity. The other was Carthage, of which we know almost nothing, except what has been told by her conquerors. The philosophy, the literature, the sculpture of Greece were preserved by the Romans because they saw that these were great; while the Punic civilization was blotted out, and a people once strong and rich, whose ships sailed to every part of the known world, whose merchants must have been among the most opulent of their day, whose military forces were able to contend with Rome for generations, and at one time almost brought her to her knees, has left no lasting contribution to human progress. Our country is far more extensive, its population, its resources, and its wealth far larger, than either of these ancient states — too large to be subdued, as they were, by a rival power; but do we want it to be a Carthage or an Athens? Do we want it to be merely big, prosperous, and comfortable, or do we long to have it great in thought, in purpose, and in moral stature? Do we in the history of our country, which has only now begun, want other peoples to ask our descendants to teach them the secret of American greatness, of the intellectual and moral energy, to which if earnestly determined this country may attain?

Whatever excuses we may have had in the past, we have none now. We are no longer a crude people struggling to overcome natural obstacles on a huge scale, a nation whose primary impulse is to expand over a wilderness. We are no longer a divided people, as when we were smarting under the wounds, yet unhealed, of the Civil War. We have not only wealth and power, but all that they can provide in the means of education and of productive scholarship. There is more danger of our suffering from surfeit than starvation. We laud the men who achieved our independence and made us a nation, and we do well, for there is no such incentive to a noble future as a worthy past; but the present alone is under our control, and we should so live in our own day and generation that our labors may bring forth fruit abundantly in the times that are to come. The men of the Revolution were said to have empires in their brains. They have bequeathed to us an empire and are asking what we shall do with it.

One thing is clear: if the nation has new duties, so has every one of its citizens; if the nation is to be great, its people must have the qualities of citizens of a great nation. They must have the aspirations, the far-reaching aims, the tenacious self-devotion required for a great design. There must be great leaders and earnest followers; and above all there must be the common recognition of a great purpose by a vast people on whom the fate of mankind will in no small measure depend.

June 15, 1930

Oh God of my fathers, and Lord of mercy, who hast made all things with thy word,
And ordained man through thy wisdom, that he should have dominion over the creatures which thou hast made,
And order the world according to equity and righteousness, and execute judgment with an upright heart.
Give me wisdom, that sitteth by thy throne.

WISDOM 9:1-4.

A BACCALAUREATE address is supposed to deal with the relation of men leaving college to the duties and responsibilities about to be thrust upon them as citizens; and so when invited to give this sermon to the graduating class I asked myself what quality in educated men the world stands most in need of today.

Knowledge has increased vastly in these later generations, and is now growing at a rapid rate. Many laws of nature, previously unsuspected, have been revealed by scientific labors; the history and condition of man, his thoughts and impulses, have been explored; until much that lay concealed has become the common property of all civilized peoples. More knowledge, no doubt, is needed, and all glory to those who seek and find it; but it is not the gravest need of mankind now.

Education, or rather the possession of the tools for getting it, is more widely diffused than ever before. For the mass of our people we need, not so much more, but better, instruction. A lack of education is not the salient mark of our time.

Intelligence is not in general deficient; and of energy and enterprise, the motive powers that make intelligence effective, there is, in our country at least, an abundance.

In spite of the cynic and the pessimist; in spite of much misconduct public and private; in spite of the prevalence of crime in our land; there is much virtue and public spirit. The observation of a lifetime has led me to believe that these qualities have not diminished, but on the whole have gained in strength; certainly that has been my impression of college students. Virtue in the community at large is often ill-directed. No doubt there is much iniquity in man; but militant virtue seems to be more commonly and more fiercely directed against a different belief about what is right than against intentional wrongdoing. The self-righteous often expend more fury upon one another than upon sinners. A lack of virtuous impulses does not appear to characterize the present generation.

To many people it may seem overstrained, but to me one of the greatest, if not the most salient, defects of our day is the lack of wisdom. Cruel and disastrous wars have occurred throughout recorded history, but none that has involved so largely the whole population, or has been so widely harmful, as the World War. The apologists for each belligerent explain that their side was not responsible therefor, and did not want it. Probably a majority of the people in every country engaged did not desire to have the war break out. Certainly a very large majority everywhere today regrets that it did; and while they may believe that for their own nation it was unavoidable they lament the conditions that made it so; and yet there was not wisdom enough in the world to prevent it.

Mankind is now seeking how to preclude war. Almost everyone is anxious for this; but no sensible man is perfectly sure that what all men object to doing they will not do. If we felt sure that wars would not come we should not talk so much about preventing them. They need not occur if there were wisdom enough to direct the course of human conduct. Someone here is thinking that he knows how war can be prevented; and so am I. But your next neighbor does not agree with you, or me, about the remedy; and to say that he lacks wisdom is simply to pass the blame, and prove the proposition that there is not wisdom enough in the world. "Ye suffer fools gladly seeing you yourselves are wise" is a statement of universal application.

To take another example: In this country there is an amount of crime abhorrent to the vast majority of our citizens. The deeds of violence, the robberies and murders that one reads of daily in the press are committed, or condoned, by a wholly inconsiderable fraction of the people. We discuss the psychological and social aspects of the matter; but if there were wisdom enough in the community one cannot doubt that crimes which almost all men reprobate would be less frequent. We should be so wise as to discover the causes and remove them.

Again our people are now sharply at issue over the question of prohibition, and its various effects upon society; but surely the traditional sage observer from some distant land, or from another planet, might ask whether if men were truly wise they would not search without heat or prejudice for the best interest of the community as a whole, until they agreed on such matters.

Personal wisdom in the conduct of private affairs is not deficient, although it is, of course, unevenly distributed. There will always be the shrewd and the simple, those who succeed and those who make mistakes and come to grief. But on the whole our people prosper mightily, for they have a keen perception of their own interests and how to attain them.

The wisdom to which I refer is of a larger kind. Much of its spirit is contained in the wisdom books of the Hebrews, such as the Wisdom of Solomon, from which my text is taken, and Ecclesiasticus, or the Wisdom of Jesus the Son of Sirach. Most of these books were written later than those of the Old Testament prophets, and not being extant in Hebrew were not included in the Protestant Bible. Many people regret this today. At the end of the hymn books before you in the racks you will find many passages from them among the selections for reading at the daily morning service in this chapel.

The wisdom literature — for it is literature of a high order — deals largely with discreet and prudent personal conduct; but it also treats wisdom as a part of religion. In its highest strains it invokes wisdom as an attribute and emanation of God, such that if a man take her as a companion and guide he shall find righteousness and happiness. That is the wisdom of which we stand in need.

Such wisdom demands serenity of temper; a judicial attitude of mind; a habit of seeking what good reasons and motives, rather than what bad ones, others may have for differing from us. It demands not only a negative, but a positive, intellectual integrity, a desire to understand that which contradicts, as well as that which supports, one's own views of what is just and wise. This does not mean a colorless, but an open, earnest mind; a mind with opinions based upon wide and deep insight into ultimate realities, not upon preconceived impressions which, by the accretion of more material of the same kind, roll up, like a snowball, into a ponderous mass. Opinion is in some men too rigid; in others not substantial enough. If, on leaving a meeting of the cabinet, Lord Melbourne is rightly quoted as saying that he wished he felt as sure of anything as Tom Macaulay did of everything, he uttered a criticism of himself as well as of his colleague.

More to our purpose is the story told of President Lincoln's interview with a deputation of ministers during the Civil War. When one of them asked if it was not a great comfort to know that the Lord was on their side, Lincoln is reported to have said he was not thinking much about that, he wanted to be sure he was on the Lord's side. In matters about which honest people differ in opinion, how can we be sure that we are on the Lord's side? The answer is that we cannot; but we can strive for the attitude of mind that will make it most probable. We can seek to maintain that attitude in all our relations in life, until it becomes a second nature; and we can apply it to any questions where our opinions will count.

Another event in the Civil War shows how a man, as devoted as anyone could be to his own cause, may yet retain an open mind when the conditions change. To me the tale is of special interest because, while it has since been published, I heard it twenty-one years ago from one of the participants. On the morning of Appomattox General Alexander, the Chief of Artillery in the Army of Northern Virginia, finding General Lee sitting before the camp fire at headquarters, told him that the retreat of the army had been cut off by Union troops, and urged that orders should be given to disband and reassemble in the mountains of North Carolina. Many of the men he said could get away, and a guerrilla warfare could be kept up for many years. Lee replied that this was all true, but that the cause for which they had fought was lost, and that they ought to remember that they were a Christian people, and strive to restore civilization as best they could. He added that he was about to meet General Grant and surrender the army. Grant, on his part, had the same desire to restore civilized life, for he wrote into the capitulation that the men should keep their horses, which, he said, they would need for the spring plowing. Each of these men saw an object beyond the one that had for years engaged all his energies.

To go back to the question how can we be sure that our opinions are right: From an early period in civilization men concerned with the administration of justice learned that the best way to attain it is to have an advocate on each side present his case as strongly as he fairly can, and have a wise and impartial judge, after weighing the evidence and argument, decide between the parties. Differences of opinion on public, as well as private, questions will always exist, otherwise there would be no progress. But the public that stands outside the contestants is in the position of the judge, and should review the question with as much impartiality as possible. That is what we mean by an enlightened public opinion, the factor on which we must in the last resort rely for the wisdom that is to guide the modern state aright.

Wisdom in this sense has a moral character. It is far from the traditional wisdom of the serpent, a mean, selfish cunning. It is the wisdom personified in the dedication of the great church in Constantinople to Saint Sophia (the Holy Wisdom), the mystic mother of three saintly daughters — Faith, Hope, and Charity. It has a moral character because its nurture requires moral qualities — integrity, humility, courage, diligence — in short, all those needed for the successful pursuit of truth.

No man can have a trustworthy opinion on all public questions; they are far too many and too complex. But he can cultivate the qualities essential to the formation of such opinions, and apply them wherever he has sufficient knowledge to do so. An attitude of this kind generally diffused would save the country from many errors, and promote a steady, instead of an intermittent, spasmodic, and painful, progress. Every man who keeps his mind in this way renders in so far a service to his nation; for the calm wisdom of those who so think is often the salvation of a people. On one of the farther pillars on the Anderson bridge is inscribed another quotation from the Wisdom of Solomon, "The multitude of the wise is the welfare of the world."

In this country such wisdom is especially needed in the rising generation, because by her great growth in population, wealth, and potential power the United States has come to occupy a far more important position than ever before. Not only does this give her a larger influence over world affairs — an influence which she cannot reject if she would — but it makes her more independent of foreign thought, and, reciprocally, others more dependent upon her. The situation is like that of a man who by success attains a large importance in his community. To some extent he inevitably becomes a leader, with the responsibilities that attach thereto.

Now these considerations affect peculiarly the men

graduating from our institutions of higher learning. Few of them will be in active public life — the more the better — but all may contribute to the wisdom of the nation. A college or university like this is not endowed solely, or even primarily, for the personal benefit of its students. That is a great end, but not the greatest. If it existed for that alone there might be just cause for jealousy on the part of those who do not share its benefits. It is endowed in order that those fortunate enough to enjoy the privilege may contribute to the welfare, and especially to the wisdom, of the whole people; and the public has a right to expect such an attitude from its educated men. Nor does it make any difference whether the support comes from the public treasury, as in the State universities, or from private benefactors. In either case the funds are given on a sacred trust for the public service, and the young men whom those funds educate receive the benefit upon the same sacred trust, to employ what they have obtained to promote the well-being, and above all the wisdom, of the country.

The wisdom we need is that which considers all things from a standpoint, not only beyond the individual and local, but beyond the temporary and evanescent; that looks upon society, upon life with its intricate duties and responsibilities, from a high plane; that strives to see questions as infinite wisdom, far above all transitory and personal interests, would regard them.

June 14, 1931

. . . Wisdom is better than strength: . . .
Wisdom is better than weapons of war.
                    ECCLESIASTES 9:16, 18.

THESE words from Ecclesiastes are graven upon the memorial tablet in our Law School to Professor Strobel, who by his sage counsel probably saved a small Oriental nation from the painful process of piecemeal absorption by powerful neighbors. In our time they may well be pondered.

The present age has seen an enormous growth of knowledge. The last hundred years have added more to science than all preceding time that man has dwelt upon the planet. Young students now talk familiarly of electrons, the quantum theory, and other marvels, from a totally new standpoint compared with that of the atoms which my generation was taught to respect as the final indivisible particles. Half a century ago the knowledge of electricity was so new that a Harvard professor is said to have assured his class that, interesting as it was in the laboratory, it could never be used on a large scale.

The applications also of the control which knowledge has given men over the forces of nature have revolutionized human life. The last sixty years have seen the coming of electric light, the telephone, wireless, the film, the gasoline explosion engine, and, as its result, the automobile and the airplane. They have seen the invention of a tube more sensitive to shades of color than the human eye, more reliable than man in giving danger signals. But wisdom does not seem to have increased.

Let us not generalize too fast. In some respects there

has been an advance in wisdom; in industrial relations in this country, for example, so far as I have been able to observe them. Employers seem to me more frequently solicitous for the welfare of their work-people, more inclined to regard them as participants in a common enterprise, than when I was young; and the labor leaders to take longer views of the true interests of their followers. These relations of employer and workmen have, however, been less affected by the inventions that have flowed from the growth of recent scientific knowledge than one might suppose. They spring from the general form of industrial mass production, from the factory system, now about a century old here, and have been little changed by the nature of the objects manufactured. In this century since the factory system began we have learned something, and I hope we have made, and will still more make, good use of it.

But, in general, wisdom does not appear to have increased. At times one feels that it has diminished. This is due partly to the very gain in knowledge and invention, for wisdom is integrated experience; and we are living in a world in large part new, with little experience of the human effects of recent changes, with so pervasive a feeling of novelty that the older maxims are often thought even less applicable than they really are. In former times, when change was less rapid, men accepted without much thought principles resulting from the long experience of their forebears under conditions not materially different from their own. But now new methods make the old uncouth. Every child says "Oh, Papa, we don't do that now," and if the rate of change keeps up your children will say the same to you.

Another reason for a lack of wisdom at the present day seems to me to lie in the stage popular government has now reached. The frequent changes of the party or persons in power in all democratic countries have tended to make them take short views and feel less responsibility for the ultimate result of their actions. They cannot afford to wait until their policy matures and people can see its effect. It must approve itself almost at first sight, or they may be swept from power by a gust of popular disfavor; and in any case their tenure of office is almost invariably too short to carry out a plan requiring much time, so they tend to tinker rather than construct. I remember many years ago, when studying municipal trading in England, asking a very thoughtful radical what the final objective was in building workmen's dwellings at public expense and under public management. The number so built was far too small to be significant in remedying the lack of houses, and it appeared likely to discourage similar building by private enterprise. I asked, therefore, whether they looked forward to complete housing of the working classes by public agencies, or if not, what their aim was. He answered that they did not know. They were experimenting toward an unknown goal. That did not seem to me a farsighted view of the matter, although the policy aroused immediate sympathy and was popular.

Wisdom, both of statesmen and individuals, is closely associated with a sense of responsibility for one's actions; and the more remote the effects considered the greater the wisdom is likely to be. A man who thinks only of proximate results, or of quick successes, can hardly be farsighted or deeply wise; whereas a philosophy based upon the measureless meaning of a man's life cannot fail to beget wisdom in thought and conduct. A philosophy involving infinity is a religion, and all true religions are concerned with a conception of the infinite.

In a Commencement address here many years ago Mr. Justice Holmes remarked that life is painting a picture, not doing a sum; and we may add that the man who lives worthily has in his mind a picture or pattern of what his life may be, or shall be, and more or less consciously conforms himself thereto. Probably he will not achieve it completely. If his aims are lofty he certainly will not, for the higher they are the less will he be satisfied with what he can attain; but he will fulfill a part of them, and if that part accords with the design he will have done something very much worth while.

In short, wisdom, in both public and private affairs, rests largely upon having in the mind a pattern, conscious or implicit, that takes account of past and present conditions, yet reaches far beyond them into a distant future — a pattern clear enough to give an intuitive perception of those things which conform to, or impair, its essential principles. If a pattern is distinct the ease of seeing what agrees or conflicts therewith is astonishing, as compared with the difficulty of determining the effect of an action when there is no pattern with which to measure it. There must be not only a pattern, but also a deep sense of responsibility for carrying it into effect. This does not mean that it is changeless, for with growth of knowledge, deeper insight, and experience in life it should be constantly modified and improved.

Someone will say that this is all very well for a Hindu Brahman who needs little food or clothing and has few cares to prevent him from sitting cross-legged on the ground contemplating abstractions; but we are in a busy, rushing world where we have to live as we must and do the jobs that are set us. To which I reply by asking if we are squirrels in a rotary cage spinning around without a purpose? Does our work take so much of our time that we have none left to think about the import of what we are doing? Are we like the man who drove so fast that he could not decide where he was going; and are we so restless that all our spare moments must be devoted to being amused by frivolity? To frame a working pattern for life does not take a vast amount of time, but it does require an earnest conscience and a sincere attitude of mind.

But, apart from excuses drawn from the temper of the age, it is not uncommon for a man to think that if he had larger opportunities, like someone better favored than himself, he would accomplish more, and be able to live on a higher plane, instead of being so restricted as he is by the narrow circumstances in which his lot is cast. He knows that he has no lack of public spirit and personal benevolence — albeit, perhaps, in a negative way — but he has never had a chance to give them effect. He has never been able to escape from drudgery into the greater things that he might do. No doubt there is much truth in this; but on the other hand it is also true that opportunity is often made, or seized, by men, rather than thrust upon them.

The guardians of the cathedral at Florence had an irregular block of marble which the sculptors declined to use because it was so ill-shaped that they could not make their designs fit into it, until Michelangelo saw in the block the figure of young David as he went forth to fight with Goliath, and hewed him out of the stone. What a man carves out of the conditions of his life depends upon the possibilities he can imagine enfolded within them. Nor to be noble need they be grandiose. Character is far more worthy than fame, and a simple work well done of more enduring value than an illustrious but defective one. Much good, both large and small, has been done under handicaps that would have been fatal without great force of character. If there is any pursuit that more than others requires good eyesight it is history, with the vast amount of sources that must be consulted; yet two of the most eminent American historians, Prescott and Parkman, were both almost blind, and the latter throughout his mature life a sufferer. Parkman, moreover, was poor, and until his books brought an income he supported himself by raising flowering plants. So successful in this was he that after his fame as a writer had become great, Waterer, the English gardener, in visiting America, wanted to meet Parkman the horticulturist; of Parkman the historian it is said he had never heard. In his earlier life he was obliged to have his material read to him and get what readers he could. At that period his French manuscripts from Canada were read to him by schoolgirls who did not know the language, or how to pronounce it. In his autobiography he says that after some years the doctor allowed him to use his eyes in reading one minute at a time, which was a great help. In his case accomplishment came from a pattern, for in boyhood he determined to write the history of the American forest, which meant that of its denizens, the Indians, of their contact with the English and French settlers, and finally of the conflict between these two.

All this he did from the first expeditions of the Jesuit missionaries to the conquest of Canada in the Seven Years' War.

Happy is the man who, like Parkman, can devote his whole life to a successful working out of the plan of his youth; but such a privilege is given to few. Many men drift, or are led, or grasp an opening into a career different from what they had intended; and yet in the transfer a pattern remains, not, indeed, of a particular work to be done, but of the man himself, of the character he wishes to have in whatever situation he may be placed. A man may hold different positions and in all of them display the same sterling integrity, firmness of purpose, industry, courage, and generosity, for such qualities can be applied in any occupation. They are above all what mark the man, and they are by no means wholly innate, but promoted and enriched by unflagging effort to rise to a pattern constantly before the mind.

I can imagine three members of this class at the fiftieth anniversary of graduation meeting together and talking over the work of their lives from which they have then retired. They will all have been men of the highest character, and have all been ultimately successful in their different lines. I will suppose one of them a man of business, another a statesman, and the third a scholar. I will also assume that they have not been at all intimate, and have been rather narrow in their sympathies — outside their own professions. The business man describes his experiences, his early luckless ventures, and his final success. Yet what pleased him most is not the money he has made, or even the sense of power that it brought, but that he has been able to supply a real want in the community, to give the public something needed for its physical and moral well-being, and above all his success in raising the standard of life and thought among his work-people. The statesman turns to him in surprise, saying he was not aware of any such motives on the part of his classmate. "We have," he adds, "fought with men of your kind and used them, and I supposed that your only object was to amass wealth. I was wrong and ask your pardon." Then the statesman speaks of his career, its disappointments, its struggles, how the best things he had ever done were the least understood, of what he had been able to do in preventing bad legislation and in laying a firm foundation for the future welfare and integrity of our public life — "not seldom," he remarks, "under bitter criticism from both of you." The scholar is now astonished, for he had thought politicians had no serious aims, save ambition to get and keep themselves and their party in office by somewhat dubious means. He too has learned something and regrets his lack of discrimination. Finally he tells of his own quest for truth, the blind alleys his researches led to, his persistence, and at last the great discovery, the work of a lifetime. The fame it brought was, of course, agreeable, but the real thing was attaining the object of his long search which would straighten men's thought, and lead them onward and upward to more truth. At this the man of business expresses his admiration, for he had thought scholars were dry-as-dusts who labored incessantly over things that no one else believed of any real use. Then the statesman says he regrets deeply they had not been in closer contact in college and in later life, for unknown to each other they had all been working at different parts of the same great pattern which their three labors had brought nearer to fulfillment, and the pattern was in the mind of God.

June 19, 1932

Then Elisha said, Hear ye the word of the Lord; Thus saith the Lord, Tomorrow about this time shall a measure of fine flour be sold for a shekel, and two measures of barley for a shekel, in the gate of Samaria.

Then a lord on whose hand the king leaned answered the man of God, and said, Behold, if the Lord would make windows in heaven, might this thing be? And he said, Behold, thou shalt see it with thine eyes, but shalt not eat thereof.

For the Lord had made the host of the Syrians to hear a noise of chariots, and a noise of horses, even the noise of a great host: . . .

Wherefore they arose and fled in the twilight, and left their tents, . . . even the camp as it was, and fled for their life.

And the people went out, and spoiled the tents of the Syrians. So a measure of fine flour was sold for a shekel, and two measures of barley for a shekel, according to the word of the Lord.

And the King appointed the lord on whose hand he leaned to have the charge of the gate: and the people trode upon him in the gate, and he died, as the man of God had said, . . .
II KINGS 7:1–2, 6–7, 16–17.

IF, WHEN you entered college, someone had prophesied that a measure of fine flour would fall to half its price, but that people would be asking themselves how they could contrive to eat thereof, men would have been as incredulous as the lord on whose hand the king leaned. Yet it has happened, not among one people alone, but over a great part of mankind.

Malthus, a century ago, frightened people by calculating that if the population of the world increased at the existing rate, the earth at no far distant date would not produce enough to feed them; and now in the temperate zone alone there is a surplus of food, and at the same time fear of starvation. The farmers are complaining that their crops are unsold, while in many countries multitudes of unemployed are being fed by public and private charity.

Now I shall not talk economics or politics because discussion of such matters in the pulpit is almost always ill-informed and futile. But it may not be useless to point out that the series of events that has occurred during your lives is not unprecedented. War, followed by material prosperity, a craze for sudden wealth, overdone and leading to distress, has happened more than once.

Let us consider the first step, that a great war is followed by a desire for material prosperity. Two hundred years ago the wars of Marlborough were followed by wild speculation in both England and France. This was the time of the South Sea Bubble in London, and Law's Mississippi Company in Paris. Fabulous fortunes were made, and then came the crash spreading ruin and suffering on both sides of the Channel. A century later it was so again after the wars of Napoleon. The cry of the Restoration in France was "get rich," and that the same thing would occur after the World War might have been foreseen and was, in fact, prophesied. In the summer of 1918 a convention of representatives of theological schools met to discuss chiefly the training of chaplains for the regiments, and a Cassandra — all prophets that descry evils afar off are Cassandras, that is, doomed to disbelief — a Cassandra told them that the war would be followed by an era of materialism and the churches had better be prepared for it. The warning fell on deaf ears.

In a more striking way the same subject was discussed that spring between two friends. One of them had a son in the army, and impressed by the lofty self-devotion of the young volunteers, he said the spirit they had acquired would so lift them that they would live upon a higher plane than their fathers. His friend replied that the war would be followed by materialism, because wars always had been. One reason for this is obvious. War causes so much waste and destruction that even in a country not ruined by the scourge there is much to be replaced, employment is abundant, and fortunes can be made.

But there is another reason for a material attitude after war, more subtle but not less powerful. It is that, like every other violent exertion, a great moral effort is followed by moral lassitude. Of this, one must beware, all the more because men are not conscious of it, and, indeed, often think their fellow-citizens in an unusually exalted state of mind. A relative of mine, enough older to remember the sentiments of young men at the close of the Civil War, in speaking of that time related how they believed that, after the slaves had been freed, all the other evils of society would one by one be attacked and abolished. Yet one of the outstanding events of the period was the shameless corruption of the Tweed Ring in New York, made possible by popular lassitude. At the same time there was great business activity, inflation and, in 1873, a collapse not unlike that which afflicts us today.

Is all this very different from what has happened during the years of your own lives? While the fighting was in progress fifteen years ago, and after it ceased, we told one another, and believed, that it was a war to end wars, that no such hideous waste of the best human lives would be allowed to occur again. We thought the world could be organized for peace, prosperity, and contentment. Prosperity came for a time in repairing the ravage of the war, and it was overdone. We were told in America that we lived in a new world where old maxims of prudence and foresight no longer applied; that universal well-being had never been so great, and that its sources were a normal condition of our new world. People lived and directed their conduct on that theory, but the structure they had built was insecure. Suddenly there came a crash, and the world-wide depression in which people stand to-day, looking blankly into one another's faces, bewildered, distraught, wondering whether business will ever recover, suggesting strange remedies, and laying the blame on someone else.

Let us not blame others, but think about the future, and so direct our course that when good days arrive we shall not abuse our opportunities, and when evil ones take their place we shall be strong to meet them. By the time you are at the helm, be it in public positions, in business, in the professions, or in any other needful work, better conditions will have come back; but, unless the past is no criterion of the future, before you lay your burdens down dark clouds will return.

Let us not blame others, but let young men prepare themselves; for such conditions are not caused by sunspots or changes in climate, nor chiefly by droughts and floods. They flow from human conduct, and hence are under human control. They arise mainly from lack of foresight, which is based upon an attitude of mind that can be cultivated, and therefore contains a moral element. Certainly so far as emotion enters into the matter, be it elation or despondency, rashness or timidity, it is not beyond the restraining power of man. If in the late war a regiment had advanced rashly, and when a counter charge came had been seized with panic, would not that have indicated a moral defect somewhere? Mind, we are not seeking to lay the blame on any person, or on any class or group of people, for almost everyone has been in the same state of mind.

About a month ago there appeared in a newspaper a short item that the editor evidently thought humorous. It purported to come from a man who wrote that an old friend of his in Wisconsin said he thought it a shame that this depression should have come right in the midst of hard times. I thought it humorous too until I began to reflect on what it might signify. If by hard times we understand the inevitable reaction that follows a period of excessive prosperity, and by depression, the despondency and lack of mutual confidence that the reaction produced, we may very properly lament the last of these results that accompanied the first. Some years ago a steamship trying to reach Boston in a fog went aground. The captain, feeling sure that he was north of his course, backed off and turned south; but as he was in fact off Marshfield he soon struck again. Running on the rocks was bad enough, but it was worse that the captain knew not where he was. Luckily the ship, with a hole in her plates, was able to creep into port.

In a sudden panic, such as sometimes occurs at a fire in a theater or when a ship sinks at sea, it must be a horrible sensation to lose confidence in everyone else, and, above all, to lose hold of oneself. At the time such panics happen they must seem like convulsions of nature where a man is powerless to stay their progress, but in fact they are made by man and can be prevented or stopped by him. We have prided ourselves as a people in not being subject to panics of that kind, and rightly so because each man has confidence that others will not lose control of themselves. A few determined men can generally stop the tumult, if the rest have some confidence in them, and every person present contributes his part in increasing or restraining the emotion of terror on which the panic rests.

All social life, all stability and progress, depend upon each man's confidence in his neighbor, a reliance upon him to do his duty. A military historian has pointed out that the practice of rapid intrenchment as developed in the last years of our Civil War, whereby a regiment protected itself from rifle fire in a few minutes, would have been impossible without confidence that the regiments on each side of it would do the same; for if either of them did not, but fell back before an attack, the intrenchment would be turned, and its exposed flank would make it useless. All mercantile credit is likewise based upon mutual confidence, and without credit, and the transactions made possible thereby, the world could not sustain its present population. If mutual confidence were absolutely destroyed mankind would sink back into utter barbarism, and in proportion as it should be lessened civilization would lose its strength, with acute suffering among all classes, greatest among those least able or willing to defend themselves.

The world is changing rapidly. Wringing from nature her secrets and thereby getting control of her forces have made what formerly seemed impossible an everyday event. They have enlarged man's power, brought the whole world into closer contacts, and opened new roads both to prosperity and to ruin, to virtue and to crime. They have made men and nations less isolated. They have made possible relief from local famine that scourged districts and destroyed their inhabitants. But they have also made the price of the farmers' wheat in Manitoba contingent upon the harvest in the Argentine, and have caused employees in Massachusetts shoe shops to lose their jobs because machinery has improved in Czechoslovakia. All this has made the major problems of life more extensive and more intricate. In doing so it has multiplied the chances of error, and the consequences that may follow. Therefore wisdom in the conduct of human affairs, and mutual confidence co-extensive with the enlarged contacts, have become more difficult and at the same time more needful. Such a need implies a duty.

So live that everyone may have confidence, not only in your honesty, but also in your wisdom and your courage. Men are not born with wisdom; they acquire it by habitual self-control, by looking not at the popular impulse of the day, but at those principles that endure and lie at the base of civilized society. The will-of-the-wisp of sudden fortunes has led away many men and women, both great and small, and has ruined multitudes beside themselves. It is often said that men learn wisdom from their mistakes, as a sailor may learn where the rocks are by striking them; but it is an expensive way of gaining knowledge, much more so than studying the chart. Wisdom is better shown before running aground than afterwards. Prosperity tries men's wisdom, as adversity tries their fortitude.

As you go forth into the busy mart of the world strive

to be sure that everything you do accords with the rights, and contributes directly or indirectly to the well-being, of your fellow men; and you will live on a high moral plane. Does this seem to you a precept excessive or unreasonable? If so, what are you in the world for? Are you here to seek pleasure and gratify ambition, or is there a moral purpose in life, and if there be a moral purpose does it not transcend all else?

Some people do not want to be better than their fellows, and dread being thought self-righteous. That is a needless fear which tends to lower the general tone and the mutual confidence among men. There are thousands who have not bowed the knee to Baal; men who live on a high moral plane and are not thought self-righteous. If you have any insight into the deeper springs of human nature you will meet them constantly in the journey of life. If you have not, you will not see them, for they do not make a show of virtue. But they have it, uphold it in others by their example, and make the world better by their presence. This College that has nurtured you expects her sons to stand among their ranks.

June 18, 1933

But when ye shall hear of wars and commotions, be not terrified: for these things must first come to pass; but the end is not by and by.

. . . Nation shall rise against nation, and kingdom against kingdom:

And great earthquakes shall be in divers places, and famines, and pestilences: and fearful sights. . . .

In your patience possess ye your souls.

LUKE 21:9-11, 19.

FEW MEN can pass through a great emotional experience without its having, at least for a time, an effect on their temperament; and what is true of persons is true also of peoples, for they are composed of individuals whose sentiments are contagious. Our passions, desires, and also our inhibitions, become more or less intense according to the feelings of those with whom we are surrounded; and with the press, the radio, and the manifest devices for spreading opinion, our contact with mankind is wider and closer than ever before.

The world has recently passed through a tremendous emotional experience — that of a war on the largest and most nearly universal scale ever known — and it has left an emotional condition of high excitability. You young men were not old enough to have felt the blind fury of the war, or, on the other hand, the devotion and heroism it inspired. But you have grown up amid the surging waves that followed the storm, and unconsciously you are under its effects. Drifting in our lifeboats, we have been lifted high on the crest of a wave, and then have sunk into the trough of the sea where we can perceive little but a frowning mass of water that threatens to overwhelm us.

We are in the trough now, and are told that the conditions of the world have suddenly changed; and that the control of man over the forces of nature, and his consequent progress in labor-saving inventions, have made him so much more productive as to raise a doubt whether he can provide for his wants. Seriously, do we not forget that such inventions, by reducing the need of human muscular strength, have made possible a large output without the slavery deemed necessary for the industry of the ancient world? Do we not forget that the state of inventions is not very different from what it was four years ago when we were told that it had brought our country to an economic plane so high and so solid that grave industrial depressions would not occur again?

Drowning men catch at straws, and suffering people are ready to seize upon any remedies proposed. A tale is related of a man on a sinking ship who thought first of saving his beloved watch from the wreck and did so by throwing it overboard. We are told that things must change, and so they must. Otherwise life would be monotonous, and men's best energies would be unstirred. Without progress in human affairs, imagination would suffer the atrophy that always results from disuse. History is the narration of a series of changes, often for the better, but not always so; and sometimes what appeared at the time grievous has proved in the end a step in the march of progress, sometimes not.

Considering the changes that have come in the past, and the delight people take in studying them, is it not strange that they have been so little foreseen? If they had been, would they not have taken a different and probably a better form? For our blind humanity foresight is difficult, and yet it is the most precious of all the gifts to men. What has happened during the last four years might have been more nearly foreseen than it was. If it had been, the worst results would have been forestalled, and we should not now be so badly off. Joan of Arc was asked by her judges what she would have done if her voices had foretold that on a certain day she would be killed or captured; and she replied that she would not have gone out to the battle that day. In view of her belief in the prophetic character of her voices, her answer was illogical, but it was sensible, for human affairs are far from wholly beyond human control. The old adage, to be forewarned is to be forearmed, has its counterpart that to be taken unawares is to be defenseless, for lack of foresight entails the happening of the unexpected, and often an attempt to meet a startling emergency by hasty and ill-considered remedies.

There are, indeed, events that we cannot foresee, and can neither prevent nor avoid. Many years ago my brother was in an earthquake in Japan, and afterwards remarked that in such a case one must hold on to oneself, for there is nothing else to hold on to. That is true of social as well as natural cataclysms. When the things about us are shaken, when the familiar landmarks are displaced, and the supports we have leaned upon are no longer solid, one must hold on to oneself. Too often that is the first thing with which a man loses touch. Too often he lets go of himself to follow the swaying of the rest, and, when he should be a steadying influence, helps to rock the boat. Too often we cast our responsibility upon others, and think if we move with the crowd we cannot be blamed, for the fault is theirs and not ours; and who is the crowd but ourselves and other timid folk of the same unstable caliber?

Deadly easy is the path of imitation, of drifting with a current; and many there be who think themselves independent because they go with a group of friends in any new direction that it chances to take. A tale is told of a Frenchman in 1848 who was asked why he followed the crowd to the barricades where they were doomed to defeat, and answered that he must follow them because he was their leader. Often we are not aware whether we are leading or following, when in fact we are both, impelled by an impulse we have received from others without knowing it, and quite as unconsciously drawing others after us toward safety or misfortune. But our ignorance of what we are doing does not relieve us of all responsibility for our conduct or our opinions, for to think aright to the best of our capacity is not only a very grave obligation to ourselves; but also to those dependent upon us, to those who may be influenced by us, and to the community of which we form a part. Burke rightly said to the electors of Bristol that he owed to them not only his vote in Parliament, but also his judgment.

Changes must take place in human affairs, sometimes violent ones, and they are not seldom carried too far; but the excesses in such cases are due in part to those who oppose all change, and not less to those who cannot see, or dread to resist, the excess. There are criteria above the impulse of the moment. Of old it was said that the Spirit would reprove the world of sin, and of righteousness, and of judgment, by which was meant our sin and the righteousness and judgment of God. Too often we take it to mean someone else's sin, our own righteousness and judgment by popular vote.

Truly, in times of public distress or excitement, the salt of the world are those who hold on to themselves, and do not run after every Lo here! or Lo there!; who keep their calmness and balance of mind, striving to see things in their true proportions, undistorted by prepossessions, and on the other hand by fear, by hallucination, or the outcries of an impulsive multitude. Sometimes in a shipwreck, or a fire in a theater, great loss of life has been prevented by a few brave men who have not lost their heads; and no one can ever know how much his own deliberate opinion may help in avoiding a calamity.

We are told that conditions having changed, with them ideas must change and former principles become obsolete. That is only partly true. In days of stress more than in uneventful times one must endeavor to distinguish between the enduring and the temporary, between the things essential to the framework of every good human society, and the expedients useful for the moment, not letting these impair the permanent structure. Now among the essentials are the personal characters of men. All society is based upon a confidence that others will do their duty, avoid offenses, obey the laws, and perform their obligations; and we maintain public officers and courts, with magistrates and judges, to secure these observances among men who do not conform of their own free will. Military discipline has for its object mutual reliance in all parts of the force, for if that is seriously impaired the army becomes a mob, doomed to defeat by any organized enemy; and in the same way if the general confidence of men in their fellow-citizens were enfeebled, society would go backward; if it were entirely lost, society would disintegrate.

But obedience to law is not enough to keep society at a high level. There is needed also a personal standard of conduct beyond that which can be enforced by law, a rectitude, a benevolence, a self-respect, that are not temporary but eternal qualities. The cardinal virtues — justice, prudence, temperance, and fortitude — are not evanescent, nor can they ever become obsolete. They have been the same since man became a rational creature, and must continue so long as he is a moral being. Their application may change, but not their essence or their obligation.

Let us strive to free ourselves from prejudice and selfishness, both personal and corporate, of interest and of occupation; for mankind can and will learn to direct itself for the general welfare if it does not lose its moral qualities and its sense of right and wrong. Above all, let us bear in mind that a good citizen's first duty — mark you, by no means his only duty, but his first duty — to the public is to preserve untarnished his own moral integrity.

Eternal Father who seest everything that we do; from whom our thoughts are not hid; grant that these young men may never forget that they live in Thy presence; so that when for each of them the star against his name marks the coming of the night, he may have the only true reward — to have Thee say: "Well done, good and faithful servant."